Advanced Praise for
LOVING SOMEONE WHO IS DYING

"Few people are as amazing as Brianna Oas Strand. In fact, everything about her was BriMazing! In *Loving Someone Who Is Dying*, her husband Nicholas Strand shares the story of her lifelong battle with cystic fibrosis and how she transformed her life into a vessel for helping others to the very end. Nothing could be more inspiring."

— Tyler R. Tichelaar, PhD and Award-Winning Author of
Narrow Lives and *The Best Place*

"No matter what troubles you have in life, Brianna Oas Strand knew that if you choose your attitude, you create your life. This amazing woman created her own destiny, refusing to let cystic fibrosis do it for her, and now this book tells her incredible story. *Loving Someone Who Is Dying* is destined to become a classic about hope, inspiration, and the human drive to go on despite all odds."

— Patrick Snow, Publishing Coach and International Bestselling
Author of *Creating Your Own Destiny* and *Boy Entrepreneur*

"In *Loving Someone Who Is Dying*, Nicholas Strand offers the truth about what it is to live with a deadly disease and to love someone who suffers from it, but beyond the facts, Nick shares truths about the human spirit, about how love never dies, and how we always have a choice about how we deal with adversity."

— Nicole Gabriel, Author of *Finding Your Inner Truth* and
Stepping Into Your Becoming

"In this book, Nicholas Strand gives an honest look at what it is like to love and care for someone who is dying over many years. We expect to hear about the hardships of such an experience, but *Loving Someone Who Is Dying* is surprisingly different because it shares his wife Brianna's extraordinarily positive outlook on life. Her story shows that even in the worst situations, we can find joy, hope, and a reason to go on."

— Larry Alexander, MA

"Many people with cystic fibrosis, and their families, are aware of their own mortality from the time they are infants. This is the story of Brianna Strand, an extraordinary woman who lived a life of joy, love, resiliency, and advocacy in the face of a mortal disease. Every person who encountered Brianna—friend, doctor, or acquaintance—leads a richer life for having known her, and she is an ongoing inspiration to us all."

— Ajai Dandekar, MD, University of Washington
Adult CF Clinic Doctor

"I love this—choosing your attitude. I think it is such an important message. I believe it is our choice to decide how life impacts us. Not always easy, but a choice. I was challenged to choose after the tragic loss of our first child, Jackson. I never imagined the possibility. And we entered a new world. We navigated in the fog of loss, but we knew right away that our path was to be parents, and we chose to continue on that path. We chose to live life with the tremendous gift of love Jackson gave us and share that with our daughters. Choosing your attitude might feel impossible, but this book will inspire you and show you a possible path that you can decide to choose."

— Donna Lynn Price, Author of
Launching Your Dreams: Making WILD Ideas Happen

"Nicholas Strand has created a truly powerful legacy of the importance of quality and not quantity. Time is fleeting, and when someone you love is dying, time becomes even more precious. This poignant book shares the journey he embarked on with his wife as she battled cystic fibrosis and a superbug. Truly a heartwarming and inspiring work of art."
— Tiiu Kristina Napp, Author of *Believing in Love Again: Through the Chaos of War, New Love Rises and Transcends All Limits*

"The book cover first caught my attention, but the title, *Loving Someone Who Is Dying*, struck me. We all will at some point lose someone, but I had never thought about how to love someone who is dying. Inside the beautiful cover is a gentle love story about a terminally ill woman told through her husband's eyes as she embraces life and teaches everyone who knew her the power of love, strength, optimism, and prayer. A lovely story and lesson about what it takes to truly enjoy each day as it comes, despite the odds, and to love fiercely, without fail."
— Michael Gross, Author of *The Spiritual Primer*

"Death is uncomfortable, yet no one escapes it. Our time is limited here on earth, but what if you were given an expiration date? What would you do with that time? It's a familiar plot in movies, but in real life, how do you navigate that time? *Loving Someone Who Is Dying* is a compassionate story of love, commitment, dedication, and hope. A story of how one woman made the world sit up and listen and navigated the time she was given to teach and touch those in her life the importance of truly living."
— Mariel Maloney, Author of *Shifting into 9th Gear*

"The power and beauty of *Loving Someone Who Is Dying* is bound to bring comfort and peace to anyone who has experienced deep grief. Touched by his own great loss, the author generously shares his experience, not shying away from what is difficult for most people to understand. He conveys universal insights for anyone who genuinely wants to support someone in their loss."

—Susan Friedmann, CSP,
international bestselling author of
Riches in Niches: How to Make it BIG in a Small Market

"Your attitude is a choice and ultimately determines your altitude and how far you rise in life. Nicholas Strand tells the humbling, inspiring, and impactful story of his late wife Brianna, who truly mastered her fate. A story that leaves a legacy, providing courage and inspiration to others for generations to come."

—John Webster, Mindset Coach
and Author of *Mastering Your Fate*

LOVING SOMEONE WHO IS DYING

CHOOSE YOUR
ATTITUDE
CREATE YOUR
LIFE!

NICHOLAS STRAND

AVIVA
PUBLISHING
New York

LOVING SOMEONE WHO IS DYING
Choose Your Attitude, Create Your Life!

Published by:
Aviva Publishing
Lake Placid, NY
(518) 523-1320
www.AvivaPubs.com

Address all inquiries to:
Nicholas Strand
Choose Your Attitude, LLC
Hello@ChooseYourAttitude.org
ChooseYourAttitude.org
LovingSomeoneWhoIsDying.com

Editors: Larry Alexander and Tyler Tichelaar, Superior Book Productions
Cover Design: Don Melendez, DM Creative and Susan Ogilvie
Scrapbook: Don Melendez, DM Creative and Brittany Burns
Interior Book Layout: Michelle VanGeest, Nicole Gabriel
Cover Photo: Jim Oas, Brianna's father

Every attempt has been made to properly fact check and tell the story as it happened.

ISBN: 978-1-950241-55-2

Library of Congress: 2019918571

Printed in the United States of America

Choose your attitude,
create your life!

always,
Brianna

SPECIAL DEDICATION

Mom,

Thanks for teaching me the meaning of love, true love, which comes from the heart. Through your lessons, you allowed me to express my true feelings, be open to communication no matter the severity, and always revert back to love in the most difficult times.

You gave me a foundation that allowed me to have the most beautiful relationship a human could ever ask for!

Love you infinity times infinity!

Your Son,

Nick

DEDICATION

To the amazing Brianna Strand,
my best friend, the love of my life, and a superhero to so many.

Brianna's biggest dream was to leave a legacy. She wanted to be remembered as an inspiration of infectious power and to continue to influence others through her amazing journey. She made living look so easy and beautiful, and she made loving look divine, all while fighting one of the toughest battles a human can face.

This is her story—her legacy. I was blessed to be part of it, and doubly-blessed because I get to help her legacy live on forever.

Forever and always, Brianna! Love you so very much, and miss you like crazy, my sunshine!

Sincerely with all my love,

Mr. Moon

ACKNOWLEDGMENTS

None of the following memories would have been possible without the constant drive and fighting spirit of all of Brianna's amazing nurses and doctors, who helped her and so many other patients prolong life and flourish to the fullest in the time they had. Much of the work done by these skilled and caring practitioners occurs behind closed doors and sometimes goes unnoticed. But not by our family. Our gratitude for what you do for humanity is beyond belief. To think that you do this for an ever-evolving list of patients—who in the end, finish their journey much sooner than most—is amazing, yet you continue forward and keep doing what you do, and we want to thank you for that. Truly, if it wasn't for doctors….

Specifically, we wish to thank:

Seattle Children's Hospital
Bonnie W. Ramsey, MD
Rob Gibson, MD, PhD
Susan G. Marshal, MD
Margaret Rosenfeld, MD, MPH

UW Pulmonary: Seattle
Moira L. Aitken, MD, FRCP
Ajai A. Dandekar, MD, PhD

UW Infectious Disease: Seattle
Paul S. Pottinger, MD at UW Medical Center

Thank you also to the outstanding support staff at both hospitals. You make all the doctors do possible. Brianna wouldn't have been able to keep such a daunting bacteria at bay and share twenty-nine years with all of us without you. For that, we are eternally grateful, and we thank you for your strength, dedication, and perseverance.

CFers (people with cystic fibrosis) and anyone fighting medical, emotional, and physical struggles, this book is for you. Brianna had no greater joy than going beyond her vulnerability, standing in front of the world, and screaming "I can! We can!" with every single one of you in mind. Her voice was amplified through your words, even those of who had a hard time speaking, as she listened to all your stories. She truly felt if she could kick CF's butt, maybe some of that energy would help others fight as well and change the meaning of CF to Cure Found.

Dr. Pottinger, Infectious Disease Specialist, was Brianna's business partner, her field marshal, working with her to conquer cystic fibrosis and her microbacterium abscessus. Dr. Pottinger, your bedside manner, strength, constant fighting spirit, friendship, understanding of Brianna's quest for quality over quantity, and ability to listen to your patients and make them feel human, instead of like science experiments, were a huge part of Brianna's drive, passion, and overall superhuman strength to push through. You were one of Brianna's greatest advocates. Brianna never fully gave her trust to any doctor because of her independence and ownership of her sickness, but she gave you the golden key. Your word was often used as a deciding factor in her mind, and she knew in your hands, her best interest was front and center. She was always comfortable with your decisions. Although you only worked with Brianna through seven of her twenty-nine years, those years were her most difficult, and you helped her through every bit of them. Our entire family is extremely grateful to you and for your role in Brianna's beautiful journey.

Seattle Children's Hospital, UW Medical Pulmonary Adult CF Clinic and Infectious Disease, Spokane CF Clinic, and all other medical staff who were a part of Brianna's medical miracles—thank you for your service. Each and every one of you had a special place in Brianna's heart and helped empower her journey. Your constant support, care, and effort, although behind the scenes, were not unnoticed. Really, you made this story possible, kept Brianna together, and helped make her journey so beautiful.

To all doctors and medical students all over the world, your daily tasks are simply part of your job, a scientific experiment; however, the real legacy of your work is saving humanity. From general practitioner doctors to nurses to home care to brain surgeons, your work is about preserving life, or when that is not possible, providing comfort. Many whom you work with ultimately lose their battles, but you preserve them through extreme dedication, spirit, and working long hours. You continue to press on and never give up, no matter how difficult or emotional a case may be. We appreciate you, your families, and everyone around you who takes pride in your career.

Staff of the National CF Foundation and Seattle CF Foundation, your energy is relentless. You were all huge supporters of Brianna, even during the difficult transitions. Having such a huge support system behind her and all your efforts motivated Brianna. The entire foundation is a blessing to everyone living with cystic fibrosis and remains an inspiration to all other foundations and support systems around. Brianna loved to share her passion for the CF Foundation, for the assistance you give patients with medication, how you help people navigate various issues, and most importantly, your infectious drive to make CF stand for Cure Found!

Brittany Burns, your relationship with Brianna was beyond any power I could explain. It was an absolute joy seeing the two of you together. From the love you shared with Brianna, to your everlasting friendship, the joy you brought her was infectious. She felt your laughter and strength. Our lives can get busy, but you were always there for her, and after she passed, you were there for me. You and Brianna often greeted each other with, "Hey, best friend," because you were. You are a huge part of Brianna's legacy, and I hope that is a source of comfort for you. For me, your support has been crucial. Your always being there for her and for me has been a blessing. You have been my strength post-Brianna, as we share common memories. I know Brianna and her amazing ways set this up—another blessing Brianna left us for our repairing us. From the start of our relationship, to after she passed, she constantly told me to go to you if I ever needed someone to talk to. And you have truly shown and exemplified to me what a true friend is. For that I am grateful.

Jim, Val, Kristen, Justin life is difficult for anyone, but even more difficult when your daughter or sister is born with an illness that seems like the end, a disease that took a village to manage. Your support never went unnoticed. But even more powerfully, your family's ability to bring laughter, positivity, and hope into some of the darkest times gave Brianna an energy that was completely unstoppable. You never left her side; you were always there for her, for us, for the family. Her legacy lives on, and it is in part your legacy; she was always the daughter you raised. It was an honor to be a part of that, and it made me value her love that much more!

Mom, Dad, Chad: My life was developed by the lessons each of you taught me. They made me a very diverse human being, and I am forever thankful for your love. You taught me the true meaning of earning my own life—to never give up, to always believe in my crazy dreams, which meant the world to me. You reminded me constantly to think of what I say before I say it, and to think of what I do before I do it. You encouraged me always to think of how others may see things, and to always challenge my own personal views. When I brought Brianna into my life, into the family, you provided overwhelming love and support, either by helping while I was on the road, or simply going the extra mile to be part of all the BriMazing that occurred. You have raised me into the man I am today, and I am forever grateful!

Road Family—Filament Productions Team, Matt Monahan, Barry Claxton, Alan Hornall, and all of my road family I have ever worked with: Life has been a journey. People don't realize our jobs put us all together randomly, challenging us all to get along while living together for a long period of time. We have the same common goal: to build a successful show day in and day out. At times we struggle, sometimes bumping heads with our ever-so-diverse personalities, everyone doing the best they can to manage life on the road. For some, it's a passion; for some, it's just work. For us all, the mission is to make it back home with a paycheck to be with those who mean the most to us. No matter what, constantly, our efforts are gifted when the lights go dark, and we are reminded of the 10,000+ individuals paying to try to escape reality for a couple of hours.

Every person I have had the honor to work with on the road, no matter our struggle or difference in personality, has challenged me to become a greater human being, making me challenge myself in creating a more diverse character. Thank you for your understanding and love, especially as life got difficult; life on the road became the only thing that remained normal, remained constant post-Brianna. An industry that sometimes seems to lack heart provided an understanding that was overwhelming and filled with warmth and love. I appreciate so many of you reaching out just to say you were there. For that, I am grateful, and I am honored to call you all road family!

Dr. Maci, Dr. Jasmin, and Clover Valley Veterinary Services: Becoming a veterinarian is a long, difficult journey. Some never make it. Thankfully, you guys saw Brianna's true passion and allowed her to live out her dream in such a short time. She may not have been a veterinarian, but being practice manager helped her surpass the role of any veterinarian. Thank you for believing in her, allowing her to be so comfortable at work, and understanding when she sometimes had to miss work when CF got the best of her. I know she wasn't there to receive her honorary degree from you, but the journey you allowed her to be part of was an honor in itself!

John Waller, North Kitsap FFA Advisor: Brianna came into the FFA program early, wanting to be just like her sister. It didn't take long for her silly personality and amazing glow to transform into the amazing leader she became. With your leadership, you guided her into one of the largest roles, sparking the foundation that lit her entire legacy on fire!

Family, Friends, and all those who interacted with Brianna and/ or me, there is just no way to include everyone—the list would go on forever: Every single one of you inspired Brianna and gave her more energy to fight. Your support and efforts gave her opportunities to share her story and legacy and grow in character as she listened. By being there, by sharing stories, you helped her infectiously spread her joy, laughter, positivity, and hope. And simply by being there, you did the same for me.

The BriMazing Book Team: This book would not be possible without the team around me! Although the story came from my heart, and Brianna's legacy, the team around me provided support, effort, and guidance to bring this entire mission and story to reality! Patrick Snow, Tyler Tichelaar, Larry Alexander, Don Melendez (aka Don Melazing), Michelle VanGeest, Susan Friedmann, Dr. Dandekar, Dr. Pottinger, Brittany Burns, and everyone else who was a part of making every single page possible—thank you! Because of your efforts, the world is a little bit better!

CONTENTS

FOREWORD

Brianna Oas Strand was a remarkable woman. I met Bri in the Infectious Diseases Clinic at the University of Washington Medical Center. She was referred to us because she was suffering from complicated, multi-drug-resistant, bacterial lung infections. Her germs were highly resistant to most treatments. And Bri had cystic fibrosis, which made her infections very challenging to treat. Over the following years, I got to know her and her family when I tortured her with antibiotics. I absolutely, positively tortured her. The medication regimens I prescribed were toxic, painful, expensive, and time-consuming. The drugs made her nauseated, interrupted her sleep, stained her skin, altered her bowel function, and made it unsafe for her to have children. Her kidneys, liver, bone marrow, and nervous system struggled to process these chemicals. One of her medicines needed to be infused by IV around the clock. For years, she remained hooked up by a subcutaneous port to a pump stashed in a fanny pack. She named it "Chuck" because she wanted so badly to chuck it across the room and be done with it. However, she talked about Chuck with good humor that bordered on affection.

Yes, I tortured Bri. I asked more of her than I had of any patient in my career. And she never complained. She never flinched. Not once. Where did such courage come from? She was a tiny thing, just a slender young woman, but she was the strongest person I have ever met. Again and again, I asked myself what I would do in her position, and every time I came up short. Her infection seemed to be under control for a time, so we decided to offer her a new treatment aimed at improving lung function, even though this meant stopping her antibiotics.

But rather than making Bri better, removing the antibiotics allowed the infection to gain the upper hand, and she never recovered, even after we restarted them. The germs roared back and consumed her body, and the flesh literally disappeared from her frame. When she died, just a few days short of her twenty-ninth birthday, her body was a shadow of its former self. Her spirit and inner core, however, remained as strong as ever—stronger—right to the end.

Her end-of-life celebration overwhelmed me. In the church foyer were scores of photos of Bri throughout her lifetime, on a variety of amazing adventures. She loved life, she loved her family, and she particularly loved animals. In time, I am sure she would have become a veterinarian. In the main hall were more artifacts of her sensational life: her wedding dress, a leather saddle, Seahawks jerseys, photos of her family. The church was filled with people who loved her: family, friends, and neighbors. I found it difficult to remain composed during the eulogy, but here is what I said:

> "Thank you for involving me in this remarkable celebration of this remarkable woman's life.
>
> I am so fortunate to have met Bri and to have helped take care of her these past years. I am part of a multi-disciplinary team of doctors, nurses, pharmacists, microbiologists, respiratory therapists, social workers, nutritionists, administrators, and others. All of us have been transformed by working with Brianna and her family.
>
> To be clear, all of our patients at UW Medicine are special. Every one of them has a unique story to tell, and unique gifts to share. And we enjoy working with all of them. But Brianna was different. She was exceptional…spectacular…unique.
>
> In the old days, doctors used to make house calls. It's a shame we don't anymore because they allowed us to experience the

richness of a patient's life, to deeply understand their circumstances, to really get to know our patients. Today, the patients come to us instead, and it puts us at a terrible disadvantage, sort of like capturing a beautiful animal in the rainforest and putting it in a sterile plastic box, and then showing it to someone and asking them to figure out its biology, ecology, and social structure, without proper context. But this was never the case with Brianna. She brought her world with her wherever she went. With Bri, you always knew who she was, what she was about, her ethos, her ethics…her personality always shone through. And it was beautiful.

When the Infectious Diseases Society of America sent out an international call seeking extraordinary patients who could brief Congress on the crisis of antibiotic resistance, I immediately thought of Bri and made the introduction. They were very impressed, and out of the entire world, they chose her for this important mission. They flew her to Washington, DC, where she briefed our nation's lawmakers alongside the leaders of the CDC, NIAID, IDSA, and BARDA. Brianna did not have to do this, but she eagerly volunteered so that others might benefit from her experience. That was typical of Bri: It was never about her; it was always about others in need. She was generous, kind, and happy to help, even while she was fighting for her own life.

I have had the privilege to work with people facing very long odds in the clinic, in the hospital, in the streets, in the mountains, and in the most austere settings. I have met my share of courageous people. But I have never met anyone as brave as Bri. She faced unthinkable difficulties with grace, dignity, and unflinching courage. And she never, ever complained.

I was not able to be with her when she died, which I will always regret. But we did speak by telephone. I apologized for failing her, and she forgave me. She told me there was nothing to apologize for, and she thanked me for the time I helped provide. She forgave me. I will never forget that....

In the end, Bri's body was no match for her spirit. But her inner core remained 100 percent strong the whole time. Yes, every one of our patients is special. But Brianna was different. We are trained in medical school to keep a certain distance from those we serve, not to get "too close" to them. This is for good reasons, and it usually works. But I came to love Brianna like a niece. She was so spectacular that I could not help it. And I am so grateful for our time together, and for the lessons she has taught me.

A day will come when I will meet a new patient facing similar circumstances. I will forge a strong bond with them, without comparing them to Bri. I owe it to Brianna to stay focused on helping every patient. I promised her I would not quit. I know a day will come when I can move forward.... But today is not that day. I am heartbroken. Remembering all of you who knew and loved her is so comforting, and so inspiring. Thank you."

In the months after she passed away, I spent time with Bri every day. This usually happened when things were quiet, or when I was driving. I would see her sitting in an empty chair, or riding beside me in the car, or standing in an open doorway. Usually she was silent, but sometimes she spoke to me in her kind, clear, confident voice. She laughed. She encouraged me to keep going, to remain focused on my practice. She praised me and thanked me for my care. She forgave me for failing her. There were times when this was simply too much for me to bear, and I fought to put her out of my mind, lest I break down during a meeting or wreck the car.

I still draw strength from Brianna, and I turn to her in times of great challenge or pain, both professional and personal. Several months after Bri died, I climbed to the highest point in Europe, the last peak of a Seven Summits quest. As we climbed higher on Mt. Elbrus, the sun rose over my right shoulder. I looked left and found our shadow stretching across the Caucasus Mountains, which stood in savage rows out to the horizon, razor sharp against the pale blue sky. It was spectacular.

And Bri was there with me, watching it, smiling. She offered me her hand. I began to cry, as I had so many times before when thinking of her, and the tears streamed down my face and collected in the bottom of the goggles, where they froze in the air intakes. I shook my head in pain, but I did not shoo her away. I wanted her there. If she could fight so hard, I could certainly do this. "Oh, Bri," I said, "I'm so sorry. We're going to be okay. Let's climb this together." And we did.

Paul Pottinger

Paul Pottinger, MD

INTRODUCTION

We are all dying. I'm dying as I write this. You're dying as you read this. But why is that a negative thing? Why is it such a tough topic?

Life is so short. We forget how complex every second is. Heart, lungs, brain…constantly working—24 hours, 1440 minutes, 84,000 seconds in a day. At any second, it could all be gone.

Each of us is a simple hourglass. We don't know when the sand is going to run out; we just know how much we have filled it with so far.

According to Webster's Dictionary, a hero is: a mythological or legendary figure, often of divine descent endowed with great strength or ability; a person admired for achievements and noble qualities; one who shows great courage; the central figure in an event, period, or movement; and the object of extreme admiration and devotion.

Now, take a deep breath. Imagine if you couldn't fill your lungs, yet never allowed that to show.

Brianna Laura Oas Strand had all the qualities of a hero. With a huge faith in God and a power beyond measure, she proved what life is all about, and crammed more into her twenty-nine years than some can fit into an entire lifetime. She led by example, never forcing her way on people. To most, she was just beautiful, powerful, comfortable to be around, and the brightest light in the room. What people didn't see was her constant inner battle with cystic fibrosis (CF) and the many complications related to it. Even after she was given an expiration date, she shattered her death sentence and proved what matters most is that we live each day to the fullest, knowing we are blessed in what we have, instead of stressing about what tomorrow may bring. CF was not disabling her; in fact, she used it to empower her!

This book is Brianna's story. I, her husband, have written it so you can understand her journey, gain awareness of what it is like to know your days are numbered, know what it is like to love someone who is dying, and hopefully, find meaning and comfort in these pages to make your own unique journey a little easier.

May Brianna's legacy live on through the help she continues to provide to you and many others. I wish you solace and joy.

Nicholas Strand

Chapter 1

STORY OF A BOY

As a kid, I was always a Garth Brooks fan. My parents bought me the kids' play microphone and guitar from Toys "R" Us. It was a tool that sparked my imagination and let it run wild. I would put a Garth Brooks CD into my parents' sound system and crank it. Running all over the kitchen, using it like a stage, with toy guitar strapped around my neck, its strings made of fishing line that did not even make a sound when I strummed them, I would belt out the lyrics to every song. As I got older, my dad started to include me in his career as an electrician, teaching me wires, and making them perform amazing things. Never having enough patience to learn an instrument, I applied those lessons from my father and applied them to my love for music—playing with a toy guitar transitioned into a DJ setup, complete with DJ CD players, mixer, and a real mic. I was hooked. Before you knew it, I was DJing family events, my brother's parties, and even a teacher's wedding.

In Bonney Lake, Washington, where I grew up, sixth and seventh grades marked the transition point from elementary to middle school. Somehow, I lucked out and graduated from a new elementary school, Liberty Ridge Elementary, right into a brand new junior high, Mountain View Junior High. In fact, we were the first class to attend.

Because it was a new school, things were still being developed, which provided me with a perfect learning opportunity. Prior to this new school, announcements had been made over the intercom. There were speakers in all the classrooms, and someone in the office would make the announcements. But the new junior high had the technology to televise them from a central room in the school.

We used a closed-circuit televised announcement system at the start of each day. With our system, teachers, administrators, and club leaders would come on to talk about their events. Students would read the schools news for the day. This was a perfect fit for me. It gave me a new focus, desire, and motivation. The school was so new that the staff wasn't sure how it all worked. With my drive and ambition, I went to work, teaching myself and slowly advancing the announcements.

The school principal and the electronics teacher saw my drive and devotion and kept feeding me. Being so dedicated, riding the bus to school didn't give me enough time to prepare in the morning for the announcements. Eventually, I convinced my dad to drop me off at school about an hour early. Then I was able to get in, slowly turn on everything, and prepare. I looked over the announcements, organized them, and planned the morning "show."

Starting with just a simple school desk and chairs, a couple of cameras, and a mic, I saw potential. The technology class was connected to the woodshop, so I went to work building a small prototype, then a full-size news desk. I created storyboards every morning for how the show was going to go, and we went live on time every day.

But like anything, eventually it was time to move on. When I transitioned into the new high school, it was time to grow.

With help from my junior high, I was guided into the Sumner High School video production class where they produced video announcements. Walking into the classroom, I saw the equipment was outdated. The system was partially working. But I had the drive and determination, and somehow, it was perfect timing because the school's audio-visual system was set for an upgrade, I worked closely with the administration and video production teacher to find the perfect system. Eventually, a brand-new system arrived—new cameras, cables, mics—and before you knew it, I was off and running.

With the new equipment in place, I turned simple morning announcements into the high school news. I contacted the local news because they used high schools as weather sensor locations, and our school was equipped with one. We were then able to collect weather graphics to include in our production. We built a green screen, and before you knew it, we had our bubbly security guard Mr. Dudley doing our weekend weather report every

Friday. I slowly advanced the announcements into a well-oiled broadcasting machine.

I did all this while attending required classes. I had science class with Mr. Pile, whose classroom was across the hall from the video productions room where I spent a lot of my time. Mr. Pile saw me often and knew of my involvement with the morning announcements and the video production class. He saw a connection between what I was doing and the Future Farmers of America (FFA). Mr. Pile was great at directing people to areas in which they could thrive. He was the school's FFA advisor—and a nationally recognized one at that.

Mr. Pile saw my passion and talents, more so than maybe I did, and encouraged me to use my talents to bring the school's FFA chapter to life through video content. He purchased a camera for me to use, so I could tag along, capturing events and creating commercials for the morning announcements, encouraging new members and acknowledging those who brought back awards. I used the footage to advertise chapter events, and even to share one of the most moving post-9/11 memories.

Prior to the horrible events of 9/11, our communication team was working with our local halal slaughterhouse, talking about diversity and agriculture. We had made many visits, attended their mosque, and talked about the religious procedure of ritual slaughter of "lawful" animals for food. But we were unaware of just how meaningful the project would be.

In the mornings, I always watched the news on the TV in my room, while my mom did the same in her room. The morning of 9/11, I was getting a late start for some reason. But I remember watching the first plane hit—the pure shock of it. I told my mom to watch, and as we both drew our attention to the coverage, we saw the second plane hit. We were filled with confusion, turmoil, and sadness…. We still had school that day, but the TV was left on in most classrooms. We also had something special: footage of local Muslims just being normal people. Our Sumner FFA team was shown working directly with them, coming together to understand. We had captured the experience, so naturally, I started editing, and the communication team and I worked together to build a video that played the next day, sharing what we had learned, the strength of community, and how we need to respect diversity—all in reaction to the events. This simple competition project turned into an important lesson on diversity.

Because of my involvement in FFA, I was known in the chapter and later became known at the state level. I was enlisted at the state level to help the team create a video. It was my calling and passion. My skills and drive were growing and morphing. I did the video for them, and the next year, our chapter's past president became state president. When he asked me to be involved, naturally, I ran with it.

When I graduated, the Washington State FFA office hired me. I attended college at Washington State University, where the convention was held every year. I worked with state officers making videos for the start of each session at the state convention. The video would play as an introduction to the officers before they came on stage to start each session.

As this process progressed, I took over stage design…video, audio, lights…and also helped with the script, working to make each session run flawlessly for the officers and spectacularly for the 3,500 statewide members who came hoping to walk across that stage with a win. By my third year of college, I was mapping out the entire event from pre-production planning with the officers to planning videos, shooting, editing, and scripting them, going over everything, planning each session, and making sure all the tech was set up.

As always, the end of the school year was bittersweet. You leave your friends, but you also finish a year. The same was true with the state officers. They became family. We would work together for an entire year, pouring our hearts into making the convention the best it had ever been, always topping the year before so the members had great memories to go back home with. School would finish; I'd walk right into the convention; then I would pack up and head back home to the West Coast, living with my parents for the summer.

The start of my senior year, the team felt different. Everyone worked together so much better. We had a very strong team vibe. The dedication was at a different level, and they all wanted the same thing—to work as hard as they could. Each year was a lot of work for everyone.

For me, it was writing and rewriting scripts, videotaping over and over again, and often working through the night to complete everything. I was prepared for the work. I was used to it. But I wasn't prepared to meet the most amazing person I've ever known.

Chapter 2

SPARKS FLY FOR BLUE CORDUROY AND CORN GOLD

This year, the team had a feeling like never before. At first, I couldn't put my finger on why it was so different. Then, one night, walking back to my dorm after a meeting, this strange feeling came over me— like a special voice in my head, saying someone special was on this team, with an energy beyond just a friend.

This was weird for me. In sixth grade, I remember briefly having a girlfriend, but we were kids just having fun with the idea of playing adults. Otherwise, my brother Chad did all the dating, attended after-school parties, was the sports champion, and hung out with a group of friends. I was always too focused and driven to have time for relationships. I was learning, creating. A few times in college, I was approached, maybe hit on—I'm not really sure, being the tech nerd I am. I shut it down. I didn't need distractions. I loved what I was doing.

You see, I was doing what you'd call a directed study—creating my own college education, putting myself in an amazing position to technically direct and manage productions at the state convention. In addition, I was busy applying myself in the college's TV program—as a senior editor and member of Cable 8, the TV Club at the Edward R. Murrow College of Communication, and production manager and technical director of the annual Murrow Symposium, which would award nationally and/or internationally known figures with the Edward R. Murrow Award. So, yeah, I was busy.

Somehow, I made it all work. I would go to school by day, and every other spare minute I had would be devoted to the state convention or video production.

The FFA team's second meeting that year was at a local coffeehouse in Pullman, Washington. During the meeting, one of the officers made a joke at the expense of another state officer, Brianna Oas, who was from Poulsbo, Washington. Brianna struck me as having an energy like no one else's. I always loved having fun and being witty, and this year's team seemed to share both my drive and my love of fun. I cracked a joke in response to the other joke. Making fun of people isn't usually a good idea—you never know how they will take it—but Brianna's reaction took my breath away, and reached a spot in my heart I wasn't ready for. Is anyone really ready to start falling in love?

When I cracked my joke, Brianna instantly frowned—yet in the same breath, laughed hysterically, using every breath she could muster. Her reaction caused the group to break into an infectious, never-ending, ab-working, cheek-bulging laughter. It was such a great feeling. Simultaneously, she had been able to flash a sad face and laugh hysterically.

And her laugh was like a bright light in the room.

As the convention drew ever closer, time was creating something new, something I didn't understand, yet wanted to build. Not only were we planning an amazing convention, but I was beginning to develop something more than a friendship.

I knew there was something special about her, but it wasn't until we reached the point in planning the convention where I sat with the various officers and worked on their Retiring Addresses—the last inspirational words the officers would offer members, the message given just before they officially retired and hung up their officer jackets, and the most anticipated part of every convention—that I started to understand.

When I sat down with Brianna and went through her remarks, I knew there was something special, something beyond superhuman, something extremely inspiring about her story. I could feel an energy in her words that I had not felt in any of the others.

With a copy of her speech in front of me and a notepad in hand, I watched as Brianna began to read her speech out loud. I immediately felt the energy I'd felt at the coffeehouse. It filled my senses—giving me chills, happiness, soft emotions, and warm fuzzies, as they say. She had a sense of fragility, yet unbelievable strength. Her light was overwhelming and superhuman.

As Brianna continued, she began to share her vulnerability. As she pulled me in even closer, she embodied gratitude, empathy, confidence, and power. I tried to focus on ideas to make the speech even better, while trying to take note of lights, sounds, video displays, but all of a sudden, I found myself *feeling* throughout her speech. I was completely mesmerized.

When Brianna finished, she was nervous from delivering it for the first time and hard on herself, stressing how much she needed to strengthen it. (Most geniuses are too hard on themselves, never being satisfied with their work.) But considering the way she had written it, the way she had explained life, the way she had made you feel from beginning to end, adding anything, changing anything, could not have made it any more amazing.

A motivational speaker's goal is to inspire. As you listen, you look for a message. However, Brianna's speech was special. She was the type of speaker who, when you least expected it, grabbed you with a side hook, yanking your emotions into an even deeper feeling. Not only did she send you home with a message, but she jammed a deep emotion into it, leaving your heart and mind filled with multidimensional inspiration.

Before we knew it, it was time for the convention. Leading up to this moment, my and Brianna's connection grew; we were bonding, sparks were flying. But we remained focused on the convention.

The convention drew 3,500 members. They all wore the same thing to show unity—blue corduroy jackets, zipped to the top, black slacks or black skirts, white collared shirts or blouses, with a blue tie or scarf. As everyone settled in, we knew everything we had been working on and perfecting for the last six months came down to this one moment.

Brianna's sister and brother took the stage to introduce her and welcome her retiring address. Her brother Justin started it off. The crowd was silent with anticipation as Justin said:

> Inspiration. A person can be inspired by a variety of things. For me, it's my baby sister. She's more driven than anyone I know and full of passion. What you may not know about her is she has contagious laughter. She has one of those silent, red-faced, I'm about to burst kind of laughs. And she uses that laughter to attack whatever life brings her way…. I love you, Bri.

Justin stepped away from the lectern as his and Brianna's sister Kristen continued the introduction:

> What is Bravery?
>
> **B**ravery is the possession or exhibition of courage and endurance.
>
> **R**adiance, bright with joy, shining with rays of light.
>
> **I**ntelligence, being quick to comprehend, being characterized by quickness of understanding and good judgment.
>
> **A**ctivity, characterized by energetic work.
>
> **N**imbleness, moving with ease and quick to understand.
>
> **N**obility, possessing the moral and mental character of excellence; and
>
> **A**llegiance, loyal and faithful.

Take the first letters of all seven of these words and they spell Brianna. You may know her by one or many of these definitions. I know her as my best friend and little sister. It is my pleasure to introduce you to your 2006/2007 Washington State FFA Secretary Brianna Oas with her retiring address titled "Days Go By."

The podium light went out, the crowd screamed in applause, encouraging and empowering Brianna even more to set aside her nervousness, relieving the pressure of all this work, channeling it into this one moment. She was standing ready on the side of the stage, as I stood at the front of the house, calling the cues so everything would go perfectly behind the scenes.

As the lights went down, a huge, black widow spider was displayed on the projection screen behind the stage. Simultaneously, the stage lights turned green—Brianna's favorite color. The song "Black Betty" by Ram Jam supplied the beat. The crowd stood with excitement as Brianna walked out with poise, dancing in front of everyone like it was no big deal—all five feet, two inches of her standing in the middle of the stage, the spotlight making her huge smile radiant, graciously putting her body into a boogie. After about thirty seconds, the song faded and she laughed as the crowd continued to cheer her on.

As the crowd drifted into silence, Brianna started to speak, filling the room with inflection, ownership, and a message of inspiration:

I hate spiders! I don't care how big or small they are, if they're five feet away from me, above me, or, God forbid, they're actually on me—everything about them gives me the heebie jeebies. So, it's no surprise that one day, right before Christmas break, Brooke and I had an incident.

We had just gotten back to her house and no one was home. I was sitting in the living room, and as she headed into the kitchen, I heard a scream. I jumped up from the couch and ran to where the noise was coming from. There Brooke was, not even in the kitchen, for above the doorway, there was a huge, hairy spider perched on the wall.

After we both stopped screaming like little girls, we started arguing back and forth about who was going to get on a chair and squish it. Well, of course, I wasn't going to, and Brooke was feeling the same way, so we opted for plan B.

Brooke ran and grabbed a can of hairspray and a bottle of Febreze. I took the hairspray, and against my better judgment, got on a chair and started spraying it at the monster like I'd never sprayed before. Brooke did the same from the ground with the Febreze, only she had a shoe in the other hand to smash the spider when it fell.

But the spider didn't fall. It started crawling, and we started screaming again.

(Brianna paused as a scream was played.)

I began spraying even harder as Brooke ran out of the room and grabbed some Lysol spray. I grabbed the shoe and kept spraying, while Brooke was now loaded in both hands, the right with Febreze and the left with Lysol, both aimed at the intruder.

Within about a minute or so, the spider began to fall. At first, only two of its legs wouldn't stick, but as it started to die, all of its legs gave out, and it fell to the ground. We both screamed and ran away again; then we rushed back to make sure it was dead, continuing to spray it, just to make sure.

Neither of us wanted to touch it, so we left it there and just warned people about it when they got home and had to walk past it.

Needless to say, this was just one of my many encounters with the eight-legged, hairy, creepy, crawly monsters that are also known as spiders.

Besides spiders, I'm deathly afraid of the dark, not a huge fan of heights, and horror movies are just not my cup of tea. I may be baring my soul here, but I'm sure at least a few of you know what I'm talking about or can sympathize with fears of your own. As I've gotten older, though, there is one fear I have that doesn't give me the willies, but it definitely makes me think.

That fear is time.

No, I'm not afraid of a clock. What scares me is not having enough time to live my life. The days go by, and time keeps ticking—that's a fact we all have to accept. But there are so many things I want to do, goals I want to achieve, so many places I want to see, differences I want to make, and so many people I want to make an impact on.

What happens if I run out of time?

Time holds many meanings in multiple situations for all of us, but no matter what, it is always steady and unfailing, as the clock ticks away the seconds, minute by minute. It is said that in the first eight seconds of meeting someone, your impression has been made. Throughout history, one second has had irreversible effects—a decision made while driving in a NAS-CAR race, an answer in an interview or contest, your ride on a bull or bronco in a rodeo or navigating your vehicle on the freeway in Seattle. Just one second determines a lifetime of possibilities and how they will be spent. With sixty seconds in a minute, 3,600 seconds in an hour, 86,400 seconds in a day, 604,800 seconds in a week, and 31,536,000 seconds in a year, you'd think I would have plenty of time to do both the things I want and the things I need to do.

But then I turn on the news and hear about all the car wrecks, shootings, illnesses, freak accidents, and any other mishaps, and it makes me think twice. Someone else's time has run out, and I wonder, *Would they be satisfied with everything they've done in their life? Would they change a second of it, if they could?*

The summer before my sophomore year in high school, I met Miles at our local county fair. He was a year older than me, a true towhead, and was considered an all-around guy. He was captain of the wrestling team, showed pigs in the FFA, worked at Dairy Queen, and was loved by all. We became friends, and even though I didn't hang out with him on a regular basis, I got used to seeing him at the horticulture site, fairs, and other FFA activities.

One night, the February of his senior year and my junior year, he was driving home from his girlfriend's house at about 10 p.m. They think he was changing a CD, but for whatever reason, he crossed the center line and hit an oncoming truck. Miles was killed instantly, less than two miles from his driveway and two months shy of his eighteenth birthday.

Although we will never forget Miles and all our wonderful memories of him, what I think of most is how he lived his life. He never went without a smile on his face; he had the biggest heart of anyone I knew, and he was so dedicated to everything he put his mind to. Miles knew what he wanted out of life, and he didn't let anyone or anything stop him from enjoying every second of it.

Most of all, he never feared time. Although he only had a little over 543 million seconds in his life, a great deal less than many who live until they're eighty, he lived every day with purpose and had a full life.

Knowing Miles, even for just a few years, an impact was made on me about the importance of the quality of life rather than the quantity. Life has a certain ending, but an uncertain timing. Each of us can make our own personal choice of how we spend the time we have!

Ever heard the saying "Live like you were dying" or "Live like there's no tomorrow?" Although true, these words are a little too cliché. For me, living life to the fullest is best defined in a poem by Linda Ellis called "The Dash." She wrote of a man who stood to speak at a funeral of a friend. He referred to the dates on her tombstone from the beginning…to the end. He noted that first came the dates of her birth and spoke of the following dates with tears. But he said what mattered most of all was the dash between the years. For that dash represented the time she spent on earth, and now only those who loved her knew what that little line was worth.

It's so easy to say, "I'll get to it tomorrow" or "I'll do it when I'm older!" You know what happens to people's enjoyment of life when they make excuses? A "but" gets in the way, and I don't mean the one that's sore from sitting right now. The kind of "but" I am referring to is the "I'd like to try that, *but*," or "I've always wanted to do that, *but*."

The next time you catch yourself using one of these phrases, re-member Keith Urban puts it best in "Days Go By"—about how we can make plans for the future, but we can't count on having a future, so today is the only time we have and we have to make the most of it. What did you do today? How did you spend your time? Maybe you competed in a contest, maybe you sup-ported members of your chapter, maybe you practiced for a contest tomorrow, or maybe you made plans to meet some new friends after this session! Whatever you did or will do tonight, are you making the most of the state convention? To make the most of every second, to add worth to that little line that's your dash, take advantage of every situation you are in!

Don't fear time. But how do you really do that? How do you live a full life, day by day, second by second?

Ask yourself, "What's my motivation? What gets me up in the morning? What activities do I do on my day off?"

For me, my motivation is living with CF. CF, or Cystic Fibro-sis, is a genetic lung disease that has no cure—I was diagnosed with it at age three, and since that time, the reality of not living as long as others has always shaped my outlook on life. It's my motivator every day, to get up and get things done—routine or not. For a long time, I contemplated whether or not I should share about my CF. I've never liked pity from anyone, and I never wanted to be treated differently—I still don't. I decided to share this part of my life with you because it is who I am, and who I will always be. And to truly enjoy your life, you have to start with knowing who you are.

I know we've all heard the old adage, "When life gives you lemons, make lemonade." Yet many of us hear it, but don't actually apply it. Now's your chance! Will you let a "but" get in the way?

FFA members, take every opportunity, every second you can, to do what you want to do. Whether it's calling up a friend you haven't talked to in a while, taking that kickboxing class you've been thinking about, competing in that Career Development Event (an event that helps build a member's college and career readiness), running for state office, or something as extreme as skydiving.

The main point is: How will people remember your dash? Miles used to wear a shirt that read, "Miles, the Myth, the Man, the Legend." That sums up his life, his attitude, and how he lived. That was his dash! My dash?—my motivation, CF. Sure, sometimes I have a hard time breathing, I've spent a lot of time in the hospital, and I take a lot of medications—so what? Why let something I can't change affect the potential of my little line? Everyone has some sort of limitation, but it's how you view that limitation that will determine your worth and your dash! Days go by—CF is *not* going to be my "but"!

As Brianna continued to speak, the instrumental part of Keith Urban's song, "Days Go By" slowly brought volume under her words to empower her last line:

Washington FFA, life is happening now and the seconds are ticking! My fear is the unlived life—I am living my dash. How will you spend your dash?

Before Brianna could even finish, the crowd began to fill the room with applause, cheering as the lyrics picked up, perfectly planned to punctuate her final words! The lights went out as the other five members of her officer team took the stage, most in tears, full of emotions, giving each other hugs. In the background, a slideshow of Brianna's life played on the screen.

Brianna's work was flawlessly executed. She had a natural talent for speaking and inspiring. She made you feel like it was only you and her in the room. Every word was emotionally controlled, her inflections in sync; she would pause at the perfect moments, her delivery making her message that much more three dimensional. You felt as though her words came straight from the heart. All the hard work from the previous few months had paid off.

Up to that moment, I had been working with Brianna, the state officer. I had felt a strong connection to her but set it aside as the six officers and I prepared to nail this convention. Brianna and I were friends, work partners. Now, I had learned her life had an expiration date. Her daily life was more than what I had observed up to that point.

I had learned that day, but earlier in our meetings when I first heard her RA, that she had cystic fibrosis. Hearing it then, my connection to Brianna had grown into a burning desire and drive to pull off the convention perfectly.

After Brianna read the speech to me that first time, I was in awe—in shock. As she finished, I fell out of my position as technical director and fell into my human emotions. I never felt any weight; I felt empathetic, empowered, and inspired. If anything, I was setting the hook of my love deeper—into a more vulnerable part of myself at the root of my love for her. It was then, for the first time, that we talked about her CF.

After that meeting, I went back to my dorm room, heart on fire, unsure why, but certain that this woman was indeed the one. With very little thought, and almost all emotion, I couldn't wait to pick up the phone and tell my mom I was in love for the first time.

When my mom answered, my emotions rendered me speechless for a second. Never before having feelings for a relationship, having always been focused only on technology, education, and the convention, I now tried to tell my mom I was in love—a topic I wasn't comfortable with yet in my own mind, let alone ready to discuss with someone else.

"Mom," I said, "I think I'm in love."

My mom's reaction, I'm sure, was like anyone else's, maybe with a little more shock, but she could hear my love through my expression. As her heart smiled, I continued.

"She's absolutely beautiful, her spirit, her mind, her soul. But she has cystic fibrosis."

My mom's heart sank. She went from an emotional momma bear to one protecting her cub from harm.

"Are you sure you are ready for that?"

Without even thinking, I said, "You taught me to love someone for who they are, not for their physical appearance." This was just that. Everything about Brianna had completely hijacked my heart, completely smothered any negative thoughts associated with her having a terminal disease. In fact, that was part of her beauty. Becoming friends with this beautiful human being, and not letting what most would run from paralyze me, but instead empower me and give me strength, came so naturally. I gave very little thought to what I was up against and what the future would bring; I was already convinced I had found my special someone. Inspired by what was ahead, I knew little of the amazing journey and adventure our lives together would be.

As a young man, I was driven, loving, and accomplished, but still hungry for so much more. I felt like nothing could stop Brianna and me. Mom, being older and more experienced, knew better what I was walking into. At that point, I hadn't really experienced death. I had nothing to go off of. I had very little information about CF and how it would affect Brianna. I was completely blind to the reality ahead.

One of my first tests came before the convention. Brianna had to go into the hospital for routine maintenance. While she was there, we talked often via chat or on the phone, sharing pictures, etc. There was a lot of talking. Much like her, I tried not to let CF become a big deal, so when she went into the hospital, we continued our normal discussions. We didn't focus on the CF or the IVs she was tangled in. An average person couldn't even tell she was sick. Really, we just continued our friendship like nothing was amiss.

She told me these hospital stays were part of the disease. We would chat for hours sometimes. She would tell me about reading her favorite magazines, eating a pile of snacks—fruit snacks, Rice Krispies Treats, popcorn, chips, Cheez Whiz with crackers, fruit by the foot—and, of course, working on perfecting her retirement address and other projects as an Washington State FFA officer. She often paused our conversations so she could stop the snack cart or pay attention to nurses or doctors stopping in with updates. She didn't change—she was still the same ole Brianna.

To me, her comfort with the situation completely downplayed this monster I had known nothing about. Our interactions in the hospital were light. Brianna, as a person with CF, appreciated that. She noticed, and later in life, she explained it to me. She said that to most people, being in the hospital was something big, but although you can explain your situation to people, maybe toning it down a bit for a given person, as the patient, it gets old after a while. However, Brianna never let people see that explaining living with CF was kind of tedious for her. She always loved to share; she was always open to any questions about her CF. Her extreme comfort with the disease radiated onto others and made me feel she was safe. She wasn't worried, so why should I be?

I was also becoming more comfortable with my feelings for her, and it was becoming difficult to keep them to myself. As we talked, our flirting made things clearer and clearer—we were both feeling the same thing. Being with her in the hospital, talking for hours, I couldn't help expressing my feelings. I couldn't just tell her I liked her. I was too nervous and shy. The thought of telling her would make me blush, grin super-wide, and panic. As we talked, and as I mustered my feelings to put them into words, a country song came to mind.

I asked her what she thought of Clay Walker's song, "Heart Over Head Over Heels." I played the song so she could hear it. As the second chorus began, I mustered up enough courage to sing with Clay—karaoke style. I wasn't a good singer, but it wasn't about my voice; it was about the words—I could only hope it was just about the words.

I sang; she blushed, and, of course, laughed. Our hearts knew what was happening. But we had not addressed it. As she responded with a giggle, I asked her, "What if I like you? What if I think I love you?"

She knew my feelings. I'd laid it out there. I was scared.

Giggling, she replied, "I think I may feel the same."

It was out. The connection we had been feeling was confirmed.

We agreed to focus on the convention, but after, we were ready to explore our feelings and see where this new adventure would lead us.

Note:

Video Archive of Brianna's Washington FFA State Officer Retiring Address is available at **ChooseYourAttitude.org/BriMazing.**

Chapter 3

A PRINCESS IS BORN

Brianna was a young girl from Poulsbo, Washington, a small, old Norwegian town just west of Seattle. It is near Bremerton where her dad, Jim, worked in the naval shipyard. Her mom, Val, worked at the local school district, North Kitsap. Brianna was the third child, after her sister Kristen and brother Justin. Soon after her birth on May 11, 1988, Brianna began to have asthma-like complications; she made many doctor visits due to chest infections: colds, bronchitis, and pneumonia. At age three, because of Brianna's many complications, her primary doctor sensed something more complex than simple chest infections was wrong. To get to the bottom of it, Brianna was brought to the Seattle Children's Hospital to see Dr. Bonnie Ramsey, a lung disease expert. Dr. Ramsey had barely settled into the room before she gave the family a diagnosis, later tests proving her correct. Brianna had cystic fibrosis. In Dr. Ramsey's thirty-plus-year career, Brianna was the only one she had ever diagnosed. Dr. Ramsey said the disease would most likely take Brianna's life prior to her thirteenth birthday. Brianna was born with the odds already against her, and this knowledge was a lot for her family to accept. In 1988, the disease was fairly new and unapproached. In 1982, a group had been formed to address the disease at universities, but no major identification of the exact gene mutation was ever found until 1989, a year after Brianna was born, and just two years prior to her diagnosis. Up to this point, doctors were just following a medication regimen that seemed to improve the condition, instead of having a clear vision of what they were conquering. In 1989, the defective CF gene was finally discovered. Now the researchers had a target to tackle.

Cystic fibrosis is a hereditary disease that affects the lungs, sinuses, pancreas, and other parts of the body. It affects more than 30,000 people in the United States and 70,000 worldwide, with approximately 1,000 new cases a year. A protein in the body, which helps balance and manage salt, is defective. Because this protein is defective, the body struggles to manage salt, which is a huge instrument and tool in keeping the lungs and sinuses free of infection. This issue makes the lungs collect mucus, clogging the airways, and trapping bacteria or germs, which creates infection and inflammation. Because the issue is the entire body, it also creates issues in the pancreas, creating digestive issues in clogging digestive enzymes that help the body absorb food and key nutrients, creating complications in growth and trying to keep the body full of nutrients. This then creates a need for enzymes to help the digestion process in her pancreas, and salt-water nebulizers to try to break up the mucus in her lungs, just as a baseline to maintain. Requiring many hospital visits and daily meds, the fight rarely slows down. Brianna's family was faced with a game akin to whack-a-mole—a popular game at the fair where a number of moles slowly rise up. Using a hammer, you have to try to whack each mole before the next one rises up. Brianna's CF was also a guessing game, trying to treat whatever bug was the most recent upset infection. In childhood, Brianna only had a couple of bugs she had to manage directly related to her CF, so things were a little easier. Whack-a-mole had a high percentage win rate at this point, so after an occasional week in the hospital, she would be back to being a normal kid again.

However, even at baseline—when the disease wasn't creating any abnormal complications, Brianna's relationship with CF was still present. Because CF affects the pancreas, Brianna had to take pig enzymes with every meal—eight with meals and four with snacks—so a bottle of enzymes was always attached to her hip because it was necessary when eating. In addition, when her cough became more pronounced, a number of breathing treatments would be prescribed, including using a flutter. A flutter is like a wind instrument, but with a vibrating ball. When Brianna would blow into it, the ball would vibrate, causing her lungs to flutter, which would cause her to cough, often in a violent coughing attack. Coughing helped the mucus release from her lungs. The end goal was to retrieve the mucus from her lungs and have her spit it out so it had less potential for colonizing and creating infection. As a kid, it was difficult to deal with such treatments every day, and as

Brianna grew, so did her relationship with CF, the aspects of that relationship never being revealed until they had to be.

Because the disease was so hidden, sometimes it was very hard for Brianna's teachers to fully understand her situation. Sometimes they would not excuse her absences while in the hospital since nothing changed when she returned to class. But CF was an internal disease. At the same time, Brianna was a strong-willed human being. She dragged CF around with her, acting normal most of the time, so that, as with my first impression of her, you had no idea anything was wrong.

Brianna's favorite color was green, specifically, neon green. She often referred to it with a laugh as being the same color as CF, or the mucus and what she would cough up. (The colors of what she would cough up usually helped identify the level of infection.) She was always silly like that, expressing her pain with originality, humor, and unique, but fun, descriptions. She would say things like that she wanted to take her lungs out and throw them against a pop machine so she could hear them kerplop against it and watch all the mucus drain as the lungs slowly slid down the pop machine. It was her fun way to bully the disease, yet have a little fun with it.

Brianna loved to laugh, but we had to keep it under control. Her coughing attacks also complicated a simple laugh. We all love to laugh, but with Brianna, we had to be careful because a laugh could turn violent enough to trigger a coughing attack, which usually meant the laughter coming to a complete halt, while Brianna turned red and we tried to ease the chain reaction.

Driven to live her life, Brianna loved animals. While she was growing up, her family lived on some acreage and always had animals— her dad regularly surprised the family with a new critter—chickens, turkeys, kittens, dogs, horses. Brianna was well-versed in the care of animals, just like she was a professional with her CF. She loved animals, I think, more than humans. She had a special place in her heart for her furry friends. But most of all, she absolutely loved horses.

Brianna's sister was active in the local drill team and barrel racing. She often rode her sister's horse and walked it as they prepared for an event or to cool off from a run. Brianna dreamed of being a vet and horse dentist—horses were her focus. She absolutely adored them.

Like any normal kid, Brianna was always having fun and playing with friends. She gained many friends as she became more and more involved with the local Blazing Saddles 4H Horse Club and joined her FFA chapter. As with everything else, she rose quickly to the highest leadership role in whatever she did. At seventeen, she even became the Kitsap Junior Rodeo Queen.

Brianna took after her sister, developing the same interests. With her best friends since before elementary school, she became a natural leader. She introduce her best friend, Brittany, to horses, so they could remain close. Today, Brittany is a horse trainer all because of Brianna's lead. Brianna loved her friends dearly, and she inspired them.

Wherever Brianna was, her friends were close behind. Brittany and Bonnie were always by her side, often participating in the same events. They were called the three Bs or BBB.

At one point, Brianna got a jockey saddle and loved to role play as a jockey, imagining herself racing around the track on her mom's horse Marie. Marie and she became close, teaming up to qualify for the state performance team. Later, Brianna added her horse Covergirl to the team; she performed with the local drill team and competed in the Northwest Junior Rodeo with the family of horses. Brianna, her sister, and her best friends were all very involved with horses, and this really helped her love for horses to blossom.

Brianna's mom was a huge cheerleader and supporter of her events, while her dad and brother often assisted in shoveling manure and providing other horse maintenance in addition to being members of Brianna's cheer squad. The family was tight and they supported each other thoroughly, but the horses provided a great bonding opportunity for Brianna, her sister, mom, and best friends. Brianna was never shy. She was full of laughter, humor, and pure joy, and she was always driven. She even learned to juggle and ride a unicycle as part of the city's main parade, and she joined band in junior high, playing the saxophone with every ounce of breath she could. She was a well-rounded, spunky kid.

In the FFA, Brianna competed in many competitions, creating a well-rounded character and honing her leadership energy. She competed in horse events, public speaking, and food and animal science, going to district and even national level competitions, and traveling to Kentucky and Indiana to the national FFA convention.

As Brianna became more and more involved, her leadership stood out. Much like Mr. Pile did for me, Mr. Waller led Brianna into many roles in FFA. She went from leading her chapter to being a district officer, and then climbing all the way up to the Washington State FFA office.

As she grew up, Brianna began to realize she loved the numbers seven and eleven. She never gave much of a reason, other than being born on May 11. She connected with the Bible verse from

Matthew 7:11: "If you then, who are evil, know how to give good gifts to your children, how much more will your Father in heaven give good things to those who ask him!" She connected this verse to the power of prayer, and indeed, it was a huge part of her family's path to surviving her youthful diagnoses and much too short life expectancy.

Brianna attended Sunday School classes and loved them so much. She was amazing at memorizing Bible stories and Scripture. Her heart was always devoted to God. She attended many Christian camps and followed her faith; her family was close to God and relied on religion, hope, faith, and prayer to get through difficult times. Thanks to their faith, her family redirected their frustration into positive energy, starting their local Poulsbo Walk-A-Thon for CF through the Great Strides—Cystic Fibrosis Foundation.

With her family's support, Brianna often participated in research, drug trials, and many CF awareness programs. For a few years, she was a star on the *CF Make-A-Wish Telethon* on her local TV station. A year after she was diagnosed, *Time Magazine* published an article on February 24, 1992, titled "Laying Siege to a Deadly Gene"—about CF and associated medical advancements with Brianna's diagnosis at the center of the story. Brianna even spoke at a fundraising event at the Paramount Theatre in Seattle, Washington, with country music superstar Vince Gill standing next to her.

Brianna's family was busy, devoted to God, close knit, strong, and full of laughter, determination, and drive. At a very young age, Brianna was already a role model to many. Before you knew it, she was graduating from high school and becoming a Washington State FFA officer. Nothing was going to stop Brianna, not even her CF.

At age nineteen, Brianna had already annihilated her death sentence—doctors had predicted she would not live beyond age thirteen—and rolled right through it like there was nothing even weighing her down. Her life was already fully packed with experiences. Dragging CF along, Brianna did this all while standing tall, inspiring others, and leading—and all with a huge smile on her face. Most never even realized she was fighting such an inner battle.

When Brianna and I met in 2006, her lungs were functioning at 85 percent, even though only three quarters of her lungs were producing oxygen, since her bottom left lobe had already deteriorated from so much mucus and infection. Brianna was already doing extra work just to breath, let alone fight infection—and live, for that matter. At age nineteen, with more than eighteen sinus surgeries before she had graduated from high school, Brianna's body was busy—busy going through more than most, and containing a constant warzone within.

This was when I met her. As friends working on a project, I was completely oblivious to the fight going on inside her. Listening to the vulnerability she was going to share with the world during our pre-speech meetings, and her positivity about something so easy to be negative about, I was spellbound. I had fallen in love with a superhero.

Chapter 4

LOVE IS IN THE AIR

After the convention, Brianna and I both returned home—she to her beautiful home city of Poulsbo, and I to Bonney Lake, about an hour's drive south of Poulsbo. We were still just friends experiencing a growing bond, an energy brewing. Up to that point, she had been an FFA state officer and I a technical director/production manager. Going home meant putting the badges down, starting the friendship as individuals, and exploring the feelings we had shared with each other.

Brianna's birthday, May 11, fell during the convention's second session, so we weren't able to celebrate the occasion as individuals. But Brooke, one of the state officers, and I came up with a plan to surprise Brianna for her birthday. When the president was officially going to end the convention, Brianna, as the secretary, took to the lectern first to make final announcements; then she turned the stage over to the president.

"That is all, Mr. President," Brianna concluded.

The president, following parliamentary procedure, and knowing what was about to happen, turned to look directly at Brooke and said with a smirk:

"Does any member or guest have any unfinished business that should come before this session…?"

Before the president even finished, Brooke stepped up to the lectern with a huge grin on her face.

Brianna, being quick on the uptake, cleverly tried to flee her secretarial lectern, to hide in the darkness away from the spotlight.

"I do, Mr. President," Brooke began, but seeing Brianna making her break, she interrupted herself. "Brianna!" She sounded like a mother catching her kid being sneaky. Brianna froze in place as Brooke told the group, "We would like you all to sing happy birthday to your very own, 2006-2007 Washington FFA secretary, Brianna Oas! So, on the count of three, let's all sing her happy birthday! 1-2-3."

Counting down like a choir teacher, Brooke led 3,500 members in singing "Happy Birthday" as one. The fun birthday song from the skating rink played in the background.

Completely caught off guard, Brianna's face was pure red from embarrassment.

After the convention, it was time for Brianna and me to celebrate her birthday in person—on our first official date.

Seattle was mid-point between Poulsbo and Bonney Lake, so we met there. Brianna took the ferry over, and I drove. We met at the Seattle ferry dock, and I whisked her away to the Melting Pot, Seattle's premier fondue restaurant. There our hearts melted together for hours. Somehow, like no time had gone by, we realized we had been there for four hours as we dipped our emotions into words, socializing, flirting, and consuming amazing foods—we finally left to watch *Shrek 3*, a movie we both had been so excited to see; its release matched that of the FFA Convention and Brianna's birthday.

Our conversations were effortless. We never lost momentum. We never stopped. Everything felt so natural and remained that way our entire relationship. After the movie, I brought Brianna back to the ferry terminal, where she ventured back to her side of Puget Sound. Her mom patiently waited there, well past midnight, to take Brianna home, and to hear how the night had played out.

A few days later, Brianna invited me up to her family's home to celebrate her grandpa's birthday. I was very much into family—I love family—and so was she. We used the time to hang out, meet her family, and even share a few simple gifts I got her. Having just graduated from college, I didn't have much money, but I was super-excited to give her the gift I had found for her.

I had remembered all her medicine bottles—one specifically for her CF with her enzymes, the pills she needed with every meal—and had observed her hiding the bottle or being uncomfortable about pulling it out while eating group meals, snacks, etc. As a way to help keep the bottle with her, make it fun, and make it look less medicine-bottle-like, I got her a green bag with a carabiner attached to it. I think it was made to hold a camera, but it worked perfectly for the enzyme bottles.

The bag looked like a neon green, puffy jacket (her favorite color, of course) and hugged the bottle so only the lid was visible. The carabiner allowed her to clip it to her purse, bag, belt—whatever.

Brianna loved it. It hid her pills, kept her from being embarrassed by them in public, and made it easier to carry them around. Most importantly, the bag made it easier to take her meds. Who would have thought this simple gift would be so helpful? It was just one of many small gestures I made.

For anyone battling a disease, injury, or whatever, independence is huge. No one's perfect. No one likes to be reminded when they forget things. However, I knew these meds meant long life for Brianna—if she took them religiously, she would be around longer. So instead of hounding her to take them, this gift was a fun way to quiet the beast and make taking the medications a little more fun and less embarrassing, without having to remind her every day.

Here I was, a young man falling in love with *the* woman, becoming best friends with her, and at the same time learning to join in a relationship with her CF—a relationship she didn't really allow many to be part of. It's that independence thing. Those fighting tend to hold on tight. In my mind, I just wanted to help out. Make things easier. Innovate. And in the end, see her smile.

When my mom asked me if I was up for the challenge of loving someone with a terminal disease, I responded with wit, not comprehending the levity of what I said. I told my mom, "You taught me to love and not let outside things get in the way." Brianna's heart had me. Being a driven and determined individual, and having achieved many of my life goals already, I knew this was, indeed, a challenge, but one I was sure I could meet.

At this point, working with Brianna on her speech was the closest I had been to her CF, her hospital visit, and her enzymes. It wasn't something she often talked about. My understanding was limited to my observations from when we had met to go over her RA.

Completely spellbound by my overwhelming emotions over our new relationship, and having graduated from college just the week prior, I received a call to add to the ever-so-changing future. As I drove home from meeting Brianna's family, I was offered the career of my dreams. A vendor I had worked with on a couple of jobs was ready to take me on as a video wall engineer and videographer for Canadian rock band Rush. I would be the roadie in charge of the big screens we use so the people in the nose-bleed seats can see the bands. I had no idea who Rush was at the time. The band had started in 1968. I was born in 1985, so I had missed their heyday. The vendor laughed at me—everyone knew Rush.

Regardless, I was completely excited about the opportunity. It was time to prepare. I rerouted and picked up a few of Rush's albums on CD (it was 2007 so no streaming audio yet) and started listening.

Completely excited to share my news with Brianna, I couldn't wait and called her instantly. When I told Brianna about the job with Rush, she was super-excited for me. That was one thing we both did—get super-excited for each other. In fact, the size of the news or idea didn't matter; our emotions were always expressed and felt, making the smallest success seem big and exciting to share.

Turns out Brianna's dad, being a musician, was a huge Rush fan.

Not until the tour did I realize what a big name they were—and how amazing they were musically.

Brianna and I had a couple of weeks to visit before the tour. Our relationship started via a long-distance relationship, chatting through Messenger on the computer, so my being away on tour would not be a big change for us.

The tour would start at the end of May and go until October. The schedule allowed a week off about every three to four weeks. It wasn't until the first break that Brianna and I made it official and started dating on July 11, 2007. I went to her parents' house where we lay on the grass, staring at the stars, and doing what we did best—talk, including sharing our feelings for each other again.

As a planner, I constructed in my head how I could make this whole thing work. I came up with our ten-year plan. We had barely begun, but I was already sharing how we were going to make something beautiful. We made a pact with each other. She wanted to be a veterinarian, and I was starting my dream career as a roadie in charge of video with major bands. A career is one of the closest and most valuable relationships we have. We go to school to learn our profession, then enter it, and through our struggles, our career remains—even if we decide to do something completely different at some point—when the smoke settles.

I wanted to make sure that no matter what happened, we would support each other in our careers—support each other in what made us happy at the core, even if it meant a struggle along the way. With that, we could make a ten-year plan. My idea was simple: In ten years, I would become a video director, so I could be home more. She would graduate vet school, and I would buy her a large animal veterinary trailer so she could become the most amazing large animal veterinarian and horse dentist ever. Of course, we laughed through some of it, while admiring the sounds of late-night crickets and the stars, but it was all heartfelt. We sunk into each other's arms under the night sky, our future laid out. It was a fairy tale for sure.

Talking in great detail, we realized this relationship was something we both wanted—something we were ready to commit to.

As I started my career on the road, Brianna prepared to start her freshman year at Washington State University in Pullman. She moved into a dorm, while, to be closer to her, I got an apartment in Pullman.

Before I knew it, I was well into my career, with a full summer tour under my belt.

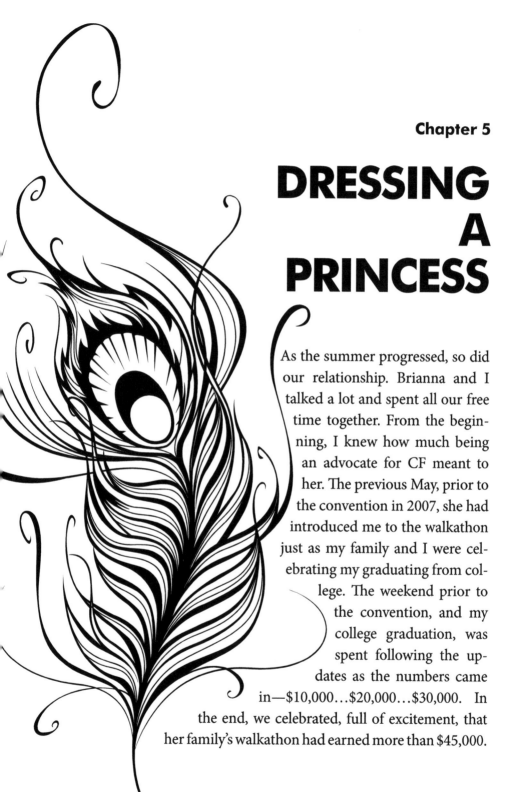

Chapter 5

DRESSING A PRINCESS

As the summer progressed, so did our relationship. Brianna and I talked a lot and spent all our free time together. From the beginning, I knew how much being an advocate for CF meant to her. The previous May, prior to the convention in 2007, she had introduced me to the walkathon just as my family and I were celebrating my graduating from college. The weekend prior to the convention, and my college graduation, was spent following the updates as the numbers came in—$10,000…$20,000…$30,000. In the end, we celebrated, full of excitement, that her family's walkathon had earned more than $45,000.

The walk was at the beginning of the year, then in the fall, annually in November, the Seattle Cystic Fibrosis Foundation has its annual gala and fundraiser, which featured an auction. It is a huge Seattle event, and one of the largest for the foundation. All kinds of business high rollers attend. All the doctors show up. Everyone is decked out in black ties and beautiful dresses. Brianna's family always looked forward to this event. Two years prior, Brianna had been the selected speaker. It was a big deal.

I found a way to be home from the Rush tour for the event—nothing was going to take precedence over it. I climbed into a black and white tuxedo. Out of the many in her closet, Brianna picked out a beautiful, navy blue dress. It didn't take much for Brianna to be beautiful. Without makeup, to me, she was already breathtaking. Then, stepping out, ready to go, hair done, makeup impeccable, and wearing the perfect dress, she was mesmerizing. If my smile wasn't big enough already, my cheeks would blush completely, giving away my feelings. It was the kind of smile that made your cheeks hurt afterwards.

She hooked her arm with mine, and we climbed into the car, headed to Seattle.

We were volunteers representing the Cystic Fibrosis Foundation. It was a great way to stay involved. We helped with the many raffles, answered questions, and took bids. After the raffle tickets were sold, a band marched through the waiting area, leading everyone into the main event hall.

Not until the bidding started did you realize how big this room really was. Companies and individuals would save a chunk of their money all year just for this event. As the bigger items were auctioned, larger sums of money were thrown down, good-natured competition pushing everyone to try to be the highest bidder.

One of my favorite parts was watching the paddles fly when the auction items were all gone—we were no longer bidding on stuff, just giving cash away. Working on the tour all summer and not having many bills, I had saved up some good money. My mom and dad joined us that night. I had talked with my mom about donating, and that I did. The bidding began…. The paddles started to fly…$100, $250, $500. I was nervous to raise my paddle, but excited to surprise Brianna and her family with my donation. Plus, it felt great to have earned it from the first year of my full-time career, post-college.

At $1,000, I raised my paddle…. What an amazing feeling it was to drop $1,000 by lifting a paddle with my number on it. The auctioneer called out our numbers as we lifted our paddles in the air. He continued: $2,500, $5,000, $10,000, $25,000…. My donation was nothing compared to what some were about to drop. People all over the room were still throwing numbers up like it was *Monopoly* money. This was when the hairs on my neck began to raise and the emotions came out. The bids went to $50,000, $100,000. This was usually where it stopped. The few who went this high were usually regular donors who set the money aside every year to donate at the gala.

After the bidding stopped, the total was announced—$1,014,750 was raised that night. Just in case the amount raised wasn't enough, a representative from Supporters for a Cure would step up and, on the organization's behalf, pledge an additional $1 million that night. More than $2 million was raised. This was a great night. Not only was it a night to be involved with raising a lot of money, but it was a fun night to dress up, to be special. For Brianna, it was a time to see all the people she usually saw in CF clinics as people, not healthcare professionals or patients—doctors, nurses, all the people around the CF environment. As always, there were a lot of people—Brianna always grew deep relationships with whomever she came into contact with. Her heroes became family, and it was always great for everyone to connect again.

Unfortunately, this happy time didn't last long. Because CF compromises your immune system, you became a breeding ground for mucus and bugs that to some people with CF could be life-changing. One person with CF could possibly be carrying and transmit a lethal bug to another patient. The foundation created the five-foot rule—a rule that was never previously enforced, but had now been made into a policy and is the subject of the recent movie *Five Feet Apart*. The danger was so real, that the foundation also created a rule that only one CFer was allowed to attend any given foundation event, walk, etc.

Being just help, not the main speaker, meant no more CF galas for Brianna. She was devastated by this situation. It was part of the psychological pain of living with CF. All of a sudden, your condition turns you away from your peers, your support group, people who really understand what you're going through. You could no longer attend an event. You could no longer talk face to face with other CFers and inspire them or help them directly—at least you weren't supposed to. No one knew what CF did to you unless you were a CFer yourself. It was a common bond. Many were excited to talk to Brianna. She had a light for everyone, even others with CF. She was always positive, always using the spotlight to lift others up.

When Brianna got the word about this new rule, she was angry. CF now controlled something. To this point, she had strangled it every chance she got, but now it stymied her. She did what she knew best: communicate. She went straight to the top to share her concern, calling the Cystic Fibrosis Foundation's national director. Brianna wanted to share her experience and her feelings and express how this new rule took her independence.

Hearing her frustration, always looking for solutions, and being proactive, I scheduled a conference call with the Cystic Fibrosis Foundation's president. I was on tour at the time, so Brianna called from home; I called from the road; Dottie Vlasuk, the Seattle chapter president called from her office in Seattle, while Mr. Bell, the president of the national Cystic Fibrosis Foundation, called from his office in Maryland. We talked for a good hour. Brianna expressed her concerns about being barred from the gala and isolated from other CFers. CF had robbed her of another form of independence.

Mr. Bell listened as Brianna shared her frustration, but it wasn't enough. He shared an experience of his own. Two CF patients were volunteering. One had caught the other's bug just by working in the same area. This interaction took that patient's life. The foundation was going to do everything it could to prevent this from happening again.

It was disappointing, but Brianna understood the reasoning, even though it was still hard to overcome.

Chapter 6

FURRY SERVICE COMPANIONS

Brianna's love of animals got the best of her, but they were her support system. She worked at the vet school where she helped clean and prepare stalls for the major, large-animal surgeries that took place at the Washington State University Veterinary Teaching Hospital. I knew it was just a matter of time before we were going to have to deal with her love of animals.

One day in the spring of 2008, Brianna called to ask if I wanted my favorite drink from the coffee place. I said yes, so she said she'd stop by my apartment with it. As she entered the apartment, she crouched behind the couch with just her head visible. Brianna and I were often silly and joked around a lot, so I just thought she was hiding my drink from me, until I heard a small animal squeal. Realizing I had heard the sound, Brianna lifted a small, adorable puppy up for me to see. My jaw dropped. He was so adorable, with black and white Collie-like markings and shorter hair, and the size of a Lab. However, no matter the level of adorable, the apartment didn't allow animals. Before I could say anything, Brianna started to guilt trip me into agreeing to keep him. She said, "Don't be mad. I had to save him from being drowned."

She didn't realize I had already made my decision. I had a heart. I loved animals. Like her, I had a soft spot for animals. No way could I be mad at a puppy. My adult side was stuck on the apartment not being animal-friendly, but otherwise, I was in love with the puppy. It was something we could make work.

Brianna had been tricked into taking him, but it turned into a blessing. One of her managers had a cow farm, and one of his dog had had puppies that needed homes. Knowing how much women love puppies, especially those working at a vet hospital, he decided to lay a guilt trip on them. When Brianna arrived at work, she was welcomed by a bunch of puppies. This particular one had stared at Brianna—it had picked her. Brianna couldn't help but fall in love. Her manager began, "Take one so I don't have to drown them." It was a bit harsh thing to say, but coming from a cowboy mentality, and to a woman melting over puppy fever, it was a solid way to get a puppy a good home. So, Brianna brought it home.

After spending some time with Brianna and the puppy, I had to head to the local coliseum where I worked as a stagehand when not on tour. That night, we had to prepare for a Dierks Bentley concert.

Brianna was always great with animals' names. Her sister had a dog named Dierks, and since I was working the Dierks Bentley show, we named him Bentley. Unbeknownst to me, Bentley would become Brianna's best friend, service animal, and really, her guardian angel. They were inseparable. Bentley knew when Brianna was sad or happy—he knew before Brianna when she was going to shed a tear, and he always lifted her up when she was down. He was her protector, so much so that a couple of years later, in the middle of the night, someone had repeatedly, aggressively knocked on our door. It was as if they were testing to see if anyone was home, or just college kids being crazy. Without a second thought, Bentley ran to the door, teeth showing, growling, barking. I wasn't home, but Bentley scared away whoever it was. Bentley and Brianna went everywhere together. Bentley never left her side, and frankly, Brianna never wanted to leave his side.

Bentley was a blessing because Brianna loved animals, and when she moved to Pullman for school, she'd had to leave behind her other animals. At WSU, she volunteered with the Professional Association of Therapeutic Horsemanship (PATH) program. PATH's goal was to provide recreational, therapeutic horseback riding for people with physical or emotional challenges. Brianna was great with horses and volunteered to care for them, cleaning stalls, exercising them, and leading the horses for the riders. But that wasn't enough. She needed more.

We talked about Brianna getting a horse. In my eyes, as a partner, I could see there was nothing better. Brianna's lungs needed exercise, but no one wants to just exercise, especially when it's continuously being pushed on you by your healthcare team. What could be better than encouraging an activity she loved, was driven to, and that helped her breathing and her lungs?

At the same time, when she rode, her energy changed. Every time she hopped into the saddle, you could tell she was experiencing a whole new feeling. She loved it. She loved the feel of her hair flowing in the wind while galloping around the arena. She'd smile wide, air flowing through her lungs. It was beautiful to see. I looked forward to it.

But Brianna didn't want just any horse. She wanted her dream horse. Finding a broke horse, ready to ride, was expensive. And Brianna wanted a challenge anyway. She wanted a baby, so we drove three hours from Pullman to pick up Dolce Blue Hancock, a beautiful Blue Roan Quarter Horse foal that had just been born and was ready to wean. It was a thrill. Brianna loved coffee, and she loved naming animals, so Dolce was perfect, and Brianna had dreamed about having a horse from the Blue Hancock bloodline.

We had to board Dolce at one of the local facilities, which was also expensive, but in my head, this was more than just a horse. It was a chance to indirectly support her in bettering her health, both mentally and physically. A horse meant care; it meant riding—and both gave her a form of independence. Plus, the physical effort she put into caring for and riding the animal was good for her. It was a natural workout for her lungs.

Still fresh in our relationship, I helped Brianna fund Dolce's upkeep. Caring for Dolce became one of Brianna's primary physical activities while in school. Morning and night, the facility fed Dolce, but Brianna made it part of her daily routine to fit in a visit. Whether it was just dropping in to give a simple treat, to say hi and give a quick hug, or bringing Dolce out of her stall to let her run or to work her for a bit, it all helped Brianna.

Being with Dolce provided an amazing learning opportunity for Brianna. She was very experienced working with horses, but she was used to ones that were already broke. She had never trained a horse from a fresh beginning, as a foal. Brianna talked with her best friend Brittany constantly on the phone about training tactics. Brianna started reading books, watching videos, learning, and perfecting training techniques. This process was great—not only did it challenge her ability to train, but it challenged her patience. Brianna was already a beautiful human being, but she always loved to improve her character; animals sense frustration and nervousness, so Dolce tested her, but they also grew close. Dolce loved to run up and get her attention, but Dolce also had enough spunk and sass to be adventurous—much like Brianna. I enjoyed watching them bond, and being part of it; I often held the lead while Brianna worked with Dolce, even creating a close bond between us.

From the beginning of our relationship to the end, Brianna and I were inseparable. When I was off the road, we never left each other's side. Being with her and being part of her working with Dolce taught me a lot. It was inspiring to watch such a small woman work with such a large animal. The lessons gave me an opportunity to apply them to working with Bentley. Together, Brianna and I learned together and applied what we learned to both Dolce and Bentley.

Dolce learned enough to be handled, worked, loved, and to advance in ground work, but not to be ridden. At the same time, Bentley excelled in his training. His desire to work just made him that much more attentive. He nailed the commands of sit, stay, and down. In addition to applying lessons from Dolce, Bentley and I went through obedience class, where he was the quickest to automatically sit when we stopped walking.

Bentley's favorite game was fetch. After working with Dolce for the afternoon, Brianna and I would often take Bentley to the university horse track, which was a wide-open field. Before the ball was thrown, Bentley knew what he had to do. He would lay down, completely focused on the ball. You could ask him to come closer or back up via voice or just hand signals. He would do it every time, but with frustration, excited to go after the ball. When we threw it, he would put all his power into charging for the ball and bringing it back, which he did every time. He was amazing.

We would take him to parks, and if any water was in sight, he had to jump in. He loved the water. During our outings, Brianna and I would walk, sit, talk, and just enjoy being together, while Bentley explored the surroundings, as our relationship continued to blossom. With Bentley, I was more of the enforcer, while he loved and protected Brianna. He was even more inseparable with Brianna than I was. The animals just naturally took to Brianna. She had that glow and smooth comfortable feeling the animals loved. She was a natural. Because of her CF and salt deficiency, her skin would be very salty; therefore, many times her interaction with animals would include being licked; we referred to her as the human salt lick. It was the direct effect of the CF mutation.

As Brianna's college years went by, my and Brianna's relationship grew tighter, building an amazing relationship.

I'm not sure why it took so long for us to marry. I was waiting for something, but I didn't know what it was. Working on the road, and being self-employed, I paid for my own insurance. Luckily, at the time, Obamacare removed the pre-existing condition exemption and raised the age limit on parental coverage from twenty-three to twenty-six. Getting married would have removed Brianna from her parents' insurance, so part of me was scared to take her off it and onto a new plan.

Not until both of Brianna's siblings and their families started talking about kids and how there's never a right time to have them did I realize that whatever I was waiting for might never come.

And Brianna was ready. Early in our relationship, she was ready. I would come across notepads where she had practiced signing her first name with my last name—Brianna Strand—all over the page, indirectly but clearly dropping the hint. Marriage was always a good topic—we would flirt as together we dreamed up plans for our big day in our future. After four years, in 2011, we decided there was no better time. I guess, as a natural-born planner, I was waiting for the perfect moment. Finally, I realized any moment standing by her side would be the perfect moment.

Chapter 7

FOREVER AND ALWAYS

In late 2010, I was on the road with the Maroon 5 Hands All Over Tour. On a day off, I hit the mall looking for an engagement ring. Always the planner, as I looked for the ring, I thought about when I was going to ask Brianna and when we should get married. With her favorite numbers in mind, I decided to ask her on January 7, 2011. I'm always being teased about forgetting dates, so I figured 1-7-11 was easy to remember. Plus, it gave us six months to plan a wedding for July 11, 2011—7-11-11, and well, use the two numbers Brianna loved so dearly: 7 and 11.

I knew the kind of ring I wanted before I started looking—nothing old, nothing too small, nothing classic, but just right. The one I bought had three huge diamonds: one large, square diamond in the middle and two smaller ones on either side. Like always, I went all out. I wanted it to pop, and it did. Brianna deserved to be spoiled; I couldn't help it. To make her smile, to glow, was my dream. And I wasn't going to do any less with her ring.

Nervous as I could be, I somehow managed to hang on to it for the couple of months before I asked her to marry me.

Dreaming of the proposal, I planned to take her to dinner at our favorite restaurant in Spokane—Clinkerdagger, a 1974 old-school steakhouse—which overlooks the beautiful Spokane Falls. It not only had a beautiful view, but also amazing food. It was a frequent date night spot for us. With the location locked down, I now had to figure out a way to surprise her with the ring.

My plan was to make a trip to Build-A-Bear, where I personalized two stuffed animals. One was a monkey wearing a blue sweatshirt, which I thought represented me, and one was a horse wearing overalls in Western fashion, which represented her. I gave them to Brianna before we left for the restaurant—I said they were something for her to hold on to and cuddle with when I was on the road. She held onto them for the drive, clueless about what was happening, carrying them with her all the way through dinner.

Being shy, I didn't want to make a scene by asking her at the restaurant. Instead, I invited her out for a walk after dinner, whisking her away to the falls. We started over the pedestrian bridge, admiring the view, the sound. About halfway across, I stopped. I asked her to look in the horse's pocket. She found the ring, and her face lit up like wildfire—her smile went past her ears, and she cried happy tears.

Before I could talk—ask the big question—she said, "Yes!"

Excited for the big day, we didn't waste a second before we started planning the wedding, and I believe we did an amazing job. Prior to our engagement, we had often talked and dreamed about our wedding, so we agreed on July 11, 2011, her favorite numbers being seven and eleven.

That year, July 11 fell on a Monday. That made scheduling easier and prices a lot more affordable. Our first choice for a venue was a place Brianna's brother's friend used for their wedding. It was private property, not a wedding venue, so we enlisted Brianna's dad to ask the owners if we could get married there. Her dad, being a socialite, was successful in booking the venue.

The couple who owned the property was ecstatic about our getting married there. It was a beautiful location, perfect for the event. The main area was an old dairy barn, painted red on the outside with huge barn doors at the entrance that welcomed you into its beauty. When you walked in, you were melted and awestruck by the history—all wood, handcrafted construction, a real piece of history. The owners showed us around, pointing out all the hardware keeping it together—it was all original wood dowels, joists, and beams. Old pulleys still hung from when men would use horses to lift heavy hay bales into position. As they walked us through, the silence made it easy to visualize it like it was happening right in front of you. Yet everything just remained untouched.

The couple allowed the women to use their own house nearby to get ready. Between the house and the barn was a small grass yard, perfect for the ceremony, that flowed nicely into the barn for the after party. Once the wedding party was ready, everyone lined up just outside the house. I waited anxiously, nervous as could be, for the wedding procession to begin. As we waited, with music playing and people settling into their seats, a rain sprinkle began, just enough to prime the nerves and boost the excitement.

In the distance, just off the side of the grassy area, random peacocks scattered. This was a gentle surprise. Our wedding symbol, love symbol, unknown to anyone on the farm, was the peacock feather. Our favorite colors, green (her) and blue (me), combined in a beautiful pattern on a peacock feather. Brianna jokingly argued it was the Seattle Seahawks' colors, but the beauty was in the peacock feather. As the beautiful birds wandered around, some perched on the fence surrounding the grass, the rain slowly let up with almost perfect timing, and it was the perfect setting to marry my best friend.

Everyone stood to attention as the procession music began. My mom and dad were in the front row with Brianna's mother. Her brother Justin escorted his wife, Erica, and Brooke from Brianna's Washington State FFA Officer Team. Then my brother Chad escorted Brittany, Brianna's best friend, and Brianna's sister Kristen. And, of course, little Rylee Jo, Brianna's beautiful niece whom she just adored, was the ring bearer.

Jim, Brianna's father, walked her down the aisle. As I saw her break the corner of the house—neon green high heels leading her step by step to me, full white dress accenting her hourglass torso, veil shielding her smile just enough to reveal the beautiful sparkle that shines and glistens with her glow—I couldn't help but weep.

My love poured over her as her dad, Jim, officiated, full of religion and Christian faith. Her father was the spiritual one, the one who shared the Bible with the family. Jim took us through the ceremony, elicited our I dos, and declared us man and wife. I lifted the veil, and we sealed our vows to love each other forever with a kiss.

Really, we had already made this commitment naturally when we first met. "Together forever and always," we always said. I called her my sunshine; she called me Mr. Moon. This day was just a way to make it official in our universe.

After we kissed, I threw a fist in the air of excitement and grinned bigger than ever. We walked back down the aisle married. Husband and Wife. Mr. and Mrs. Strand!

While everyone made their way to the barn, Brianna and I took a ride on the back of a tractor, soaking in the beauty of the day—our family close by.

The barn was decked out in amazing decor. Brianna's uncle was the DJ. In the corner was a baked potato bar complete with all the fixings. It was delicious but simple. To the side of that was a candy display with every kind of candy Brianna and I could think of. We loved our sweets, often eating our dessert before dinner.

Outside the barn, we paid homage to Brianna's love of coffee with a Mocha Medic truck. This was a converted ambulance serving espresso and award-winning coffee. Just inside the barn, to the right, was a photobooth for everyone to take crazy pictures. We also had multiple disposable cameras so people could help capture memories.

We gathered to cut the cake, which was placed on a beautiful stand a friend had built for us. We had cupcakes all around the multi-tier display. The frosting was green and blue. And in the center, we had a light pointing directly at our cake topper.

As soon as we had gotten engaged, I had dreamed up a beautiful bobble head display and worked on it for six months. UPS had barely delivered it in time for the wedding. The bobble head was Brianna and me sitting on a bench in the park. Brianna was in her wedding dress, and I was in my tuxedo, wearing a camera around my neck. Bentley was sitting between us, a paw on Brianna's leg, begging for a pet. In Brianna's left hand was a Starbucks coffee about to be stolen by Dolce, who stood just behind the bench. And in front of us were our two cats at the time, Onyx and Hemi, and, of course, Dorito, Brianna's hedgehog. As people walked by, they couldn't keep themselves from flicking one of us, keeping our heads continuously bobbling.

What a beautiful night it was. We shared our big day with family and friends and pulled it off on a small budget. One of the most beautiful things about the night was the sight of the older couple who owned the place perched on the stack of hay bales in the corner of the barn, holding hands, with grins that seemed bigger than their faces. They seemed to truly admire the love we shared. They were like a symbol of what Brianna and I dreamed of becoming.

Then it was time to whisk Brianna away. She was completely unaware of the surprise I had in store for her. She knew we were headed to the airport the next morning, but she had zero idea where I was taking her. I did all I could to keep it a secret. I loved making her smile—loved being romantic. And this was by far one of our greatest times together.

Before we left, I handed both our parents sealed envelopes. They were not to be opened until our plane had departed. The envelopes included our itinerary and contacts, and said there would be absolutely no cell phones, no communication, besides simply confirming our arrival. We made our way to our room, went to bed, woke up, and left for the airport.

I gave Brianna clues to help with packing. But nothing more than what to bring. It truly wasn't until the airport, at the ticket counter, that Brianna learned our destination: Jamaica.

Once we had our tickets in hand, we went through security, and then I shared the full itinerary. Remember me saying before that I was a planner. Yeah, I planned this out too. We'd be there for ten days, and I made sure to plan days for just relaxing on the beach at the resort, just us, and days for activities, only planning one activity a day.

Of course, however meticulous a plan may be, it can't account for planes being rerouted mid-flight. So, our honeymoon started with some hiccups. One of the flight attendants had gotten sick, so our flight was rerouted to Arizona, and we had to catch a flight to Jamaica from there. When we landed in Arizona, I got right on the phone and went to work. Somehow, I was able to book a flight that got us to Jamaica just a couple of hours after our original arrival time.

We arrived in Jamaica just in time for the sunset.

The resort we stayed at was the Royal Plantation in Ocho Rios. It was absolutely beautiful. It was a smaller resort with only seventy-five rooms, but it was part of a larger family of resorts. We soon found we were really the only people staying there, so it was just beyond perfect. It was like our own private resort.

When we got to the resort, we were welcomed by our butler, who guided us up to our ocean-view room. I asked Brianna to get dressed for dinner, which she struggled with because she was distracted by the view.

Slowly, the first night's surprise became obvious. Out the window was a beautiful view of the amazing Caribbean Sea, and just beyond a quiet, peaceful, smallish, secluded beach. In the view, you could see a long dock that extended out into the sea. At the end of the dock, Brianna spotted the surprise. I had scheduled a sunset dinner to start the trip.

As Brianna looked out over the scene, the sun was splashing new colors across the sky. The sea was roaring. The candlelight at the table become more prominent and became the light we shared. As we feasted on a private, romantic meal, I shared our itinerary for the week ahead; we talked about what had happened in the last twenty-four hours, and, of course, we talked, smiled, laughed, and loved some more. It was natural and never grew old.

The rest of the week included a dolphin experience, a trip to the blue lagoon, an amazing bamboo ride down a river, horse riding through the ocean, and lots of peaceful time on the beach. I knew the place we were staying was high scale since it had a butler, but I didn't realize the level. On the secluded beach, set aside just for Brianna and me, we found our lounge chairs. Before we could sit down, we were offered drinks, food.... It was an all-inclusive resort, so everything was prepaid.

We relaxed with drinks and then went for a swim. As we entered the sea, we took pictures and enjoyed the breathtaking beauty. When we returned to our lounge chairs, to our surprise, before we could even settle in, a staff member came to brush the sand off our feet. It was beyond relaxing.

The staff at the resort quickly became our friends. They were such warm people. Before the trip was over, our activities rep invited us to lunch and walked us down to the local market where she shared

Jamaica's fresh bammies and bought us a homemade steel drum made from a tin bucket. Because it was a small resort, not many people were there during the week, so we became extremely close to the staff, and when our ten days were up, we shared parting tears with them.

Of course, every great story has its humor. Ours was funnier to family and friends, even Brianna, than me. On our last night at the resort, we shared a romantic, lobster dinner in our room; the doors were open wide to the sea breeze, with the surf rolling in. It was perfect. But there was one more surprise, one I had not planned. When we got home, I was hit with three full days of illness due to food poisoning.

And just as I was recovering, I was hit with a staph infection from a pimple on my forehead.

And I learned I was allergic to the medicine prescribed to tackle the staph infection by breaking out in hives all over my body.

Three full weeks of misery after our amazing honeymoon passed before I finally got back to my normal self.

As if the sickness wasn't stressful enough, during that time we also bought our first car. I had a 102-degree temperature when we bought a black 2008 Lincoln MKX that would gain the name Black Betty.

With a new car, memories of a beautiful honeymoon, and being joined as one, Brianna and I ventured back to Pullman so she could continue her college education. Up to this point, her health hadn't been much of an issue. Only needing simple, bi-monthly checkups, she was an uncomplicated CF patient whose condition was kept stable for the most part with managerial meds. Early in 2012, her fifth year of college, managerial turned into more frequent visits.

In fact, Brianna's visits became so frequent that her doctor at the Spokane clinic requested we be seen at the UW Infectious Disease Clinic and Cystic Fibrosis Center. He felt there might be something more than Brianna's less complex CF issues.

Brianna had also struggled to get into the WSU College of Veterinary Medicine twice, so with these new health concerns, we decided it was time to move back to the west side of Washington.

Chapter 8

A PRACTICE RUN –MOM'S JOURNEY

I had spent nine years in Pullman—2003-2007 for my undergrad studies, and 2007 to 2012 for my love for Brianna. For me, being away from home for so long was difficult. I was ready to be closer to family. More importantly, I wanted to be closer to my parents.

As the baby in her family, and with a disease like CF, Brianna was also ready to go home. CF is a family disease. Blessed to have had the five years to create a beautiful foundation, Brianna's family was now ready to be close again. Our families missed us, so with the referral and the struggles with veterinary school, our hearts were ready to be closer to home.

Finally making it official, we set a date to move back. My family loves to help, so they made the five-hour drive to Pullman to retrieve our belongings. Somehow, we had collected a lot in just five years together, as we grew from an apartment to a house. As we conquered the packing, slowly loading the U-Haul, we noticed something was wrong with my mom.

Mom felt off. She was writing funny and misspelling words, even though she was an avid crossword puzzle master. Trying not to pay too much attention to it, we grabbed the last box, packed it into the vehicles, and broke free back to the West Coast. We caravaned with the U-Haul, Brianna in the MKX, and Mom and Dad in their car.

Mom was a heavy smoker. Before our trip back to the west side, I talked with her about quitting…reminding her how Brianna and I needed her around to be grandma to our kids someday. But sometimes it's best to let things be since, most of the time, the person is aware and struggling. They want the same thing, so sometimes it gets brought up, but when it is, it's just like ripping a Band-Aid from a healing wound. But I couldn't help it. We sincerely wanted her around.

When we made a stop during our trip over the mountain, my mom complained her legs hurt, but no one thought that was abnormal. In the early 1980s, my mom had broken her back in a car accident. And just before the move, she'd had back surgery, so pain on a five-hour drive didn't seem out of the ordinary.

We were all happy about the move and excited to spend more time together. We even talked about having Sunday meals at home with

Mom. Mom loved her family and always loved when we got together. Being away for so long, we were excited as well!

Brianna and I planned to stay at her parents' house for some time, until I got enough work to rent or buy a place. My parents' house in Bonney Lake was on the way to Poulsbo, so we stayed there overnight, instead of driving the additional hour to Poulsbo.

It was nice. We all sat down together, talked, and relaxed. My family loved Brianna—who didn't?—so my mom, dad, Brianna, and I chatted about our memories of Pullman and our dreams for our future.

It was exciting to get a sense of our new normal. I liked the idea of seeing family more often, especially after being away for nine years. Brianna was my everything; she was all I needed to feel full, complete, and content, but being around family was an added bonus. And I had been away from Momma's nest long enough that I was excited to make up for some of that time.

As the night passed on, everyone became more and more exhausted from the long day of packing and driving. Mom still did not feel well and went to bed early. We followed soon after.

When we woke, Mom was still sleeping heavily. Brianna and I left with Dad seeing us out. Mom not getting up was weird; she and Dad usually hugged us and waved us out of the driveway, but she hadn't been feeling well, and she was tired, so we didn't bother her.

With a full U-Haul and a full day's work ahead, we made the hour drive to our rented storage unit. We went right to work unpacking five years of love Brianna and I had created.

Around eleven that morning, Dad called. He sounded puzzled.

Mom was at the hospital, in a coma from a brain hemorrhage. After Brianna and I had left, Dad had headed to work. The day before had been a long day for all of us, so we had all thought Mom was just worn out. She's a hard worker and known to overdo it. Dad called her from work, but since he knew she was exhausted, he didn't think it odd when she didn't answer. Then she slept through her physical therapy appointment. When the office called, she answered, but she was slurring her words and sounded odd. In professional fashion, the office called 911 and then my dad.

We raced to Seattle to be with Mom and Dad. After many stressful hours of trying to catch up with reality, and anxious for answers, it was time to share the cause. We were told Mom had lung cancer; it was advanced—terminal. She only had a few months left.

We were crushed. Devastated.

There was light in the darkness, however. The doctors believed the clot would pass and had hope her mental acuity would return so she could have a couple of lucid months with us.

This situation was difficult in so many ways. Here we were finally moving back to spend time with family after being away for so long, and now, all that promised time had been ripped away.

This time would be difficult for Brianna because Mom had expressed many times how much she hated smoking, and she felt so guilty doing it, knowing Brianna was struggling just to keep her lungs alive. They had talked about it often. As always, Brianna had not been shy about sharing her relationship with CF. It was her way to inspire, and perhaps even convince, my mom to quit. I had hoped Brianna might change Mom's ways. Brianna struggled with anyone who destroyed a perfectly working set of lungs since she was born with a set constantly struggling to survive.

Unfortunately, it was too late. There was no looking back. All there was to do was live, no matter how much time Mom had left.

Mom had always been there for me, so I decided to be there for her now. Thankfully, my job allowed for that. I had proven myself, so the work would come as soon as I was available to do it. This was the end of my mom's life, so I didn't want to waste a day. Work would come and go, but I only got one mom.

Mom and Dad were a mess. They struggled with the illness. They struggled with one another. They were in a bad place. Dad shut down. Being there allowed me to return what Mom had done so well for me. I took charge of her care, learning all I could about her meds and how to care for her. Throwing my organizational skills at Mom's illness helped her and Dad, but it also helped me. It was something I could do.

Processing mentally what was happening long term was hard. Instead, I focused on the short term—taking care of the acute issues, figuring out today, tomorrow. Doing all this while playing with complex medications and making sure she had food to eat—making sure I had food so I could take care of her. Holy crap, that was a lot to overcome.

Focusing on understanding the meds myself was difficult enough, let alone explaining them to Dad or anyone else who came to help. Jumping on the computer, tickling my brain, I worked to master a sense of ease in my presentation. I created a floor plan for the meds, laying them out on a grid. I made a spot for every medication, giving each bottle a letter on top for easy identification since twenty-five prescription caps are hard to identify when they all look the same. Each cap's letter was paired with its matching letter on the grid laid out on the surface.

With the grid complete, I found a home for the chart on the counter top. I dug deeper into Microsoft spreadsheets, trying to get a better sense of time. I assembled a schedule, a flow chart for each medication, and created a column for each letter associated with the bottle—the purpose, drug name, minimum time between doses—then twenty-four boxes for each hour of the day.

		PURPOSE	DRUG NAME	DIST	AM										NOON						PM		BEDTIME			
					12:0	1:00	2:00	3:00	4:00	5:00	6:00	7:00	8:00	9:00	10:00	11:0	12:0	1:00	2:00	3:00	4:00	5:00	6:00	7:00	8:00	9:00	10:0	11:0	12:0
			FOOD																										
	A	Swelling	DEXAMETHASONE																										
S	B	Stool Softener	DOCUSATE SODIUM																										
C	C	Seizure	LEVETIRACETAM	12hrs																									
H	E		MultiVitamin																										
E	G	Stimulate Bowls	SENNA-DOCUSATE																										
D	H	Neuro Pain	GABAPENTIN	12hrs																									
U	I	Acid	OMEPRAZOLE	12hrs																									
L	J	Stomach	SUCRALFATE																										
E	K	Depression	VENLAFAXINE																										
D	O	Pain (Long)	OXYCOTIN	12hrs																									
	R	Sleep	ZOLPIDEM																										
A	D	A, N, P	LORAZEPAM (Ativan)	2hrs																									
S	F	Pain (Breakthrough)	OXYCODONE	4hrs																									
N	L	Cough	GUAIFENESIN	4hrs																									
E	M	Pain (Breakthrough)	MORPHINE	2hrs																									
E	N	Nausea	ONDANSETRON	6hrs																									
D	P	Nausea	PROCHLOREPRAZINE	6hrs																									
	Q	Ocean Spray	SODIUM CHLORIDE																										
		A=Anxiety N=Nausea P=Pain (Lower Level)				NO FOOD			w Food			Whenever															

*Larger version available on page 247 and online at **ChooseYourAttitude.org/Resources**

I used a sheet for each day, using colors to help identify the hours. Red meant no, yellow meant whenever, and green meant take with food. The medications had a rotation I used to fill in scheduled times, even scheduling in three meals a day to try to preserve sanity. As meds were taken, we would X out the box so we knew when it was taken. The chart was not just for me. It was important for others coming in to help.

After organizing the twenty-five prescriptions and finally creating a system to ensure they were taken as prescribed, we could present them to her healthcare team. We would bring stacks of records to each appointment to help answer questions, constantly trying to solve the equation for a more peaceful journey.

Mom was a fighter. In her head, dying did not compute. Her confused mind held on to every little bit of false hope. In one sentence, the doctor would tell us there was no cure and it was a rapidly moving cancer, but we could try radiation; it was unlikely to work, but might slow the cancer down a bit. That idea meant so much to her, even more than the many hours of radiation she would have to endure.

As Mom, Dad, and I rode this roller-coaster ride, doing all we could to live, keep up, and simply stay fed and rested, we tried to find time to bond.

As Mom got sicker, she became more worn-out, her energy almost spent. She was more confused. Dad and I were by her side twenty-four hours a day, taking turns being on call. But always being there to help the other process decisions that needed to be addressed.

As we finally created a process, family and friends were finding out about Mom's condition. Phone calls starting coming in, people started to drop by unannounced, and family members became lost in their emotions. It's great to see people, but often the visits were for them, their sanity, not for Mom's or our sake. The influx of well-wishers added counseling others to the mix, answering the same questions over and over, trying to filter random visits to protect Mom so she could get some sleep, hiding some of the pain medications from guests who might consider stealing them, as warned by care professionals.

Dad and I were exhausted, yet we had to step out of our own emotions to convince someone crushed by Mom's diagnosis that they could not see her right now so she could sleep. Some made it through despite our protests. Mom, Dad, and I did our best to be gracious, but it was difficult at times.

For Dad and me, visitors meant more work. For Mom, they meant less sleep, less energy. And, of course, Mom had dignity. She hated people seeing her down. Who doesn't? Tapping into the last of her energy to greet those needing their last interaction was difficult. What they didn't see was her confusion, her deterioration. They asked her so many questions, and she tried to answer them. It was hard to watch and seemed to drain Mom's strength. Don't get me wrong—many of the experiences were helpful, and Mom cherished them. However, often visits left Mom exhausted and confused.

We were deep into a complex set of emotions. I was thankful to have my dad; my dad was thankful to have me. Our struggles got even more difficult as the tougher decisions needed to be made. Near the end, as the cancer took over Mom's entire body, her lungs started to give up. She had to go into surgery to remove water from the lungs to try to salvage a few more days, weeks. But surgery meant discussing Mom's DNR (Do Not Resuscitate) status. As her child, that meant admitting mom was dying, that we were at the end. As an adult, it meant the possibility of her living via a machine and eventually having to pull the plug.

The situation was tough, but for Dad and me, there was a clear choice. For my brother Chad, who was having difficulty processing the situation, it was an impossible choice. To me, the cancer had already won. It had already taken Mom's life. It was just about making the final journey comfortable. Chad, still lost in his emotions, was trying to hold on. We finally brought the surgeon in to help the family come to a common ground and make an educated decision.

This was a difficult time. Confusing.

Besides caring for Mom, I was also thinking about preserving memories. Recording her saying "I love you," convincing her to write Chad his last birthday card, and having her sit down with him to organize the many piles of random photos. As we wrote on the back of the photos, and filed them by specific year, I scanned them and transposed what was written into the file, archiving our entire photo history. As a family, it was so much fun to relive our history, to archive the past as we unintentionally prepared for mom's slideshow.

Later, I was bummed out because I missed Mom's recipes. But at least my taste buds still retain their amazing memories of Mom's cooking. After many hours at work, she would come home and make every meal from scratch, each time with all five food groups.

One of the biggest blessings, and yet a struggle to pull off, was Mom's last photo shoot. On a whim, sensing a stable part in Mom's journey, I wanted family pictures. We had been talking about getting family photos done for a few years but hadn't found the time. We were running out of time.

Brianna's dad was a photographer, and this was the perfect time to schedule him to do the shoot. Val, Brianna's mom, would assist. Plus, I really loved the idea of Brianna and me getting pictures with our parents. I picked a day, invited our entire family—my brother, Brianna's parents, Mom's family.

The morning of the shoot, we had everybody finally confirmed. However, Mom and the weather were wildcards. Luckily, the weather couldn't have been more beautiful. We shot the pictures in my parents' backyard. Mom and Dad loved their backyard—roses everywhere, fountains, grass, archway. Caring for it was a true labor of love for them. Before Mom reinjured her back, her yard and working in her garden was her chosen Zen.

At that point, with the falls running, fountains flowing, grass freshly cut, sun shining, and family showing up in their white shirts and blue jeans—we wanted something simple—Mom decided she wasn't having it. No one likes pictures when they're sick. Mom didn't want any.

In the two months of struggling with Mom's illness, Brianna and I had danced back and forth from her parents' home in Poulsbo to my parents' home. Brianna did more of the dancing, as I rarely left Mom's side. But thankfully, Brianna had stayed over the night before. Seeing mom's mood, I was stuck with canceling—and it had been a major feat to get everyone together in the first place. But using her amazing powers, Brianna lifted me up, keeping me strong and powering forward. At the same time, she gracefully stepped into my mom's room, and doing what girls do best, spent a few hours with my mom playing dress up, playing with makeup, adjusting mom's wig, laughing, socializing, and bonding. Somehow—like she did so naturally—she tucked Mom's cancer aside and made her look beautiful. Mom wore a brown dress jacket to make her stand out from the family and keep her warm, a white undershirt and blue jeans to keep her comfortable and match the family. The makeup and wig somehow pulled all the dark shadows of cancer back and replaced them with smiles and some of Brianna's glow.

Mom was transformed into a completely new person, smiling as wide as could be. The entire family ventured into Mom's beautiful yard, where we spent the afternoon laughing, giggling, and taking pictures with many variations. Success. We captured numerous pictures that day, memories, and even her beautiful smile. We would use those pictures at her funeral. This was the last time Mom made it outside and saw the whole family. It was like fate had completed its last task and was already moving on to the rest of the journey.

As the days passed and her body slowly suffocated from the cancer, Mom became sicker and sicker. Eventually, she went to the hospital where she was made comfortable. With the end drawing near, making the many trips back and forth from my parents' house to Brianna's, we noticed a cemetery—Haven of Rest, in Gig Harbor. Passing it every trip, you couldn't help being taken aback by the amazing view of the mountain, the sound, and the beauty of the spot tucked away in a quiet side of the hill surrounded by evergreens. It was the perfect spot for Mom.

It had been close to two and a half months since I'd worked. I had remained focused on Mom. It created a strain on my relationship with Brianna, as we both fought for time together. We understood each other's needs, but struggled to find a happy balance. At the same time, I was losing energy. Being by Mom's side 24/7 with few breaks was wearing on me. More so, the money we had saved was slowly disappearing. We were getting some resistance from Brianna's parents since what was presented as some time to get on our feet and build our savings for a new house turned into me spending what we had and staying with my mom. Up to that point, I had shut work off, declining any offers.

Near the end of July, I received a call about a gig at the Gorge Amphitheatre, just two hours away. The gig was doing handheld camera work for the Watershed, a country music festival over the three-day weekend. The vendor was a company I had worked with in the past. I was looking at it as a quick gig to get some money to replenish our funds and have a break away from Mom, so I accepted the offer.

With the gig a couple of weeks out, I was excited to share the news. When I told my mom, as always, she was excited for me. However, it didn't take long for her deeper emotions to come up. I had been her caregiver. Her confidant. She trusted me with everything. My dad and mom had relied on me for a lot. They leaned on me for help and support because I really seemed to be the most clear-minded of everyone, so I helped Mom and Dad make the big decisions. My leaving for this gig meant the safety barrier was removed. As the days got closer, progression advanced.

Mom was well aware of the date as she lay in the hospital rapidly declining. I had to be at the gig by ten in the morning. I had planned to leave at around six to make the two-hour drive with some padding to allow for any issues on the road. By that point, Mom had sunk into her hospital bed, and her mind had shut down; it was just a matter of time before the rest of her body would finally give up the fight. The day before, I said my goodbyes. It was hard for me. I was worn out. Handing Mom off to my brother Chad was difficult. I went back to my parents' house to try to get some rest before heading to work.

Mom's timing had always been impeccable. And that's how she went out. At two in the morning, just hours before I had to return to work, she took her last breath.

Mom was out of pain. The fight was over. And she was on her way to heaven.

The day before, I had shed my tears, painfully wept, crying as I left my mom's side for the last time. At that point, the previous two months had helped me say my goodbyes and work through my mom's absence. I still deal with the pain today, but I have come to accept my new normal. With that ease, I went to the gig, working the Watershed at the Gorge that day like Mom would have wanted me to do. I love what I do, and she never wanted to get in the way of my work.

The past few months had been a journey, to say the least. They had also been a time for reflection, and almost a practice run for what was ahead for me. We are all going to die, and because Brianna was living with cystic fibrosis, I knew our time was limited. Trying to keep Mom's memory alive, I still had to bring my focus back to Brianna. After all, the new complications with her CF had been a deciding factor in moving back to the west side of the state.

Work, for me, is a labor of love. I absolutely enjoy going to work, so the gig provided the perfect transition from being a 24/7 caregiver to doing the job I love.

Note:
For your convenience, a complimentary excel template
of the Medical Schedule Sheet is available at
ChooseYourAttitude.org/Resources

Chapter 9

QUALITY OVER QUANTITY

Caring for my mom had been extremely difficult, not only in terms of processing her sickness and death, but also because it put a huge strain on my relationship with Brianna. Thankfully, our parents only lived an hour apart so we could see each other, but the situation made for some very chaotic times, and we never really got a chance to slow down. Only the strength of our relationship, friendship, and love for each other pulled us through.

But I wasn't the only one having a difficult time. My entire family had a hard time dealing with Mom's illness. One bright spot was that my whole family loved Brianna. I could see the light she brought out in my family when she was around. As her illness progressed, Mom often leaned on Brianna to boost her mind, faith, and strength. Brianna was just so strong, relaxed, bright, and in control, and her presence made you feel comfortable—even in these severe times.

Brianna was happy being real with anyone. She was comfortable answering questions about her CF—any questions. She would be vulnerable with anyone. My mom's faith wasn't strong, and she was a smoker, so she was in a tough spot emotionally and mentally. But Brianna, like always, came to the rescue.

Completely scared to ask, nervous about which words to use, my mom asked Brianna, "How are you so comfortable with death?"

This is where Brianna's powers shined. For most, the question is extremely difficult. My mom had a lot of regret about compromising her healthy lungs over a deadly habit.

Brianna responded with a smile. Shoulders back and confident, she didn't take the question lightly, but her understanding of life, her mission, her journey, and knowledge of where she was headed were strong.

> "Every struggle I have faced has been outshined by my faith in God. My faith to be with God when I pass. I can't stress about the journey ahead, but through my faith, I am one with God, comfortable with heaven and what it means, and looking forward to that opportunity. Knowing where I am headed, knowing I am in God's hands, I am stress-free, focused on my life on earth, and driven to make every day the best I can, for I know tomorrow is a blessing."

Their countless talks were definitely a huge help in mom's struggle with leaving the earth, with the pain she felt for, in a sense, causing her own death, and with the guilt associated with that. Brianna's power made my mom comfortable and at ease. So much so that Mom got baptized just a couple of weeks before she passed.

Brianna's strength, and her drive to live every day to the fullest and not let a second go unused exemplified her philosophy of quality over quantity. She often reminded me of this idea during our many pillow talks or when she was talking to doctors. This drive helped ease my mom's struggle. At the same time, Brianna applied that drive to her daily care for her CF. In her mind, CF was a mere limitation, just a challenge. She wasn't going to let CF control or label her. Sometimes, this philosophy made her doctor visits difficult, so it was important to find the right doctor. There were many amazing individuals, many who were well recognized for their research, but Bri struggled to find those who, in addition to being scientists, valued her sanity.

On a good day with cystic fibrosis, the doctors prescribe four to six hours of medications, breathing treatments, and exercise. What happens to life? A normal day to most is sixteen hours, with eight left over for sleeping. That usually is broken up into eight hours for work, two hours preparing for work including commuting back and forth, two hours or more for eating, and if you're lucky, an hour or two to rest and relax.

Where do you add saline breathing treatments, a nebulizer, or a prolonged inhaler? This treatment has you breathe in saline in a vapor form, which then enters the lungs and, essentially, tries to replace, lubricate, and release the bugs that the salt proteins should do naturally. This is a thirty- to sixty-minute treatment. That's not including any of the meds they have you run through, or the IVs to hook up to. How's a person to live? Brianna dragged CF around, like a doll tied up with rope, never giving it a chance to stand. She was in control; absolutely no way was she going to let CF control her. Brianna wasn't a controlling person; she was just responsible, in control of her life, and knew what she wanted to do with it.

The first couple of doctors Brianna went through gave her a plan that conflicted with her routine. Instead of working with Brianna, they would hold strong. In turn, Brianna would go home and do what fit her everyday schedule. If she was going to have a day with her family and medications got in the way, she chose her family. Her meds could wait. Up to that time, her list wasn't heavy, but some of the meds, some of the chest exercises, were left out—the managerial things. Her days just didn't have enough time in them.

Finally, we met Dr. Pottinger, Brianna's true hero. Brianna had gone to a children's hospital all her life—colored walls, fun snacks, toys everywhere. When moving to Pullman, and growing past the children's hospital team that she'd had her whole life, she entered the pale white walls, strict communications, self-responsibility, and sterile atmosphere of adult healthcare. It was a hard transition. Brianna's stubborn will and drive for quality sometimes made her interactions with doctors difficult.

Before moving to Pullman, it had been pretty smooth sailing. Every three months, Brianna would go in for a checkup and adjust her meds. Rarely would she need an at-home IV tune up—a heavy punch to catch up again. Pills were usually strong enough. It wasn't until the superbug abscessus (ab-ses-sus) was introduced that the relationship with the doctors became more direct, constant, and frequent. It went from pretty easy sailing, to an unknown battle, or an extremely aggressive game of whack-a-mole. None of us were ever really able to process the severity of what was happening.

When Brianna moved from Poulsbo and the children's hospital to Pullman to attend WSU, she began treatment at a place in Spokane. Simple CF Stuff. But then things became difficult. She suffered from more frequent, stubborn colds. The superbug was identified during her fourth year at WSU. She wasn't able to get into veterinary school on the first try, but she was determined and gave it a second go. Sometimes things do happen for a reason. I think this was one of those times. Fate was in control. The doctor she had been seeing in Spokane wasn't equipped to deal with superbugs, so Brianna was referred to the UW infectious disease department. This meant also seeing its team of cystic fibrosis doctors.

Because I never wanted to get in the way of Brianna's relationship with her parents, they continued to accompany us to her appointments. CF is a family disease. Her family had been involved from the beginning, so why change a constant that had been successful for so long? Why take a resource from Brianna and the doctors for no reason?

The appointments were a real struggle. Most doctors would come in, listen to Brianna's symptoms, and then tell her what her regimen was going to be. Sometimes, she would go home with ten hours a day's worth of medications and treatments. That in itself was stressful. At times, just accepting the doctors' plan, and only doing half of the full plan, she was not left with time to live life.

Then her cultures came in positive for the superbug abscessus. Not an abscess, not abscessed, abscessus—a bug we likely all have interactions with. Most of us can expel it with our natural salt proteins. Because Brianna's were nonexistent and her body was constantly fighting infections, those infections became hosts for abscessus. Sometimes, bugs go away naturally, but sometimes, as in Brianna's case, they find perfect conditions to thrive and grow. I think the bug's name fits it since it is obsessed with creating an abscess in the body with taking over. Mycobacterium abscessus is a rapidly growing bacterium closely related to tuberculosis and Hansen's disease, better known as leprosy. The bug is found in water, soil, and dust, which is known to contaminate medical devices, some medications, and some products. Some bugs respond well to antibiotics; this one was more stubborn. We didn't know where she got it, nor did it matter; she had it. Many doctors or nurses would cringe when the name was mentioned, unable to hide their reactions. They knew what the diagnosis was.

It was time for the infectious disease doctor to take over. Luckily, Dr. Paul Pottinger was a blessing. Brianna adored him because of his bedside manner—his ability to listen not only to the symptoms, but to the person's desire to live. He knew what it meant to live, to have mental health, to have life, to have independence over the disease. Dr. Pottinger was an avid outdoors man, who loved outdoor adventure and climbed many of the world's highest peaks, including Mt. Everest; just as he conquered mountaintops, he would try to help his vast list of patients conquer their infectious diseases. Before Brianna would be given a plan, Pottinger would listen carefully, then propose a few ideas, sharing what was available and the pros and cons to each. Ninety-nine percent of the time, he would favor one that Brianna loved. He knew how much Brianna desired to maintain her quality of life. He knew if you spent ten hours a day dealing with CF, it just might prolong your life, but why? What kind of life would you have?

Before the visits were over, both Brianna and Dr. Pottinger were on the same page with a solid game plan. Both were fighting. I could see sometimes it was hard for Dr. Pottinger. But Brianna's spirit and strength meant so much to him that he built a plan they both could conquer. To leave his office feeling like she was still in charge of her disease gave Brianna an even stronger power that lifted her up even more.

Brianna's relationship with her doctors was important because she often spoke to groups of medical students. Public speaking was a natural talent for her. People listened. Her spotlight drew attention both big and small. If the crowd was just you, or if the crowd was 3,500, each and every person was glued to what she had to say.

Every year, the UW first year medical students invited her and Dr. Margaret Rosenfeld to come speak. Brianna would sit in front of about 100 or so students, all entering the medical program. It was the start of an eight-year journey for them. She would put her vulnerability aside, bring her strength front and center, and answer every question. The students asked questions about whether she feared death, her struggle around wanting to be a mother, taking her meds, and her relationship with doctors. These were the same questions Brianna and I often discussed as pillow talk.

Brianna's last words during these talks would always be her strongest asset. She reminded them, although they would be doctors, scientists to some extent, not to lose sight of the reality that their patients were humans. She reminded them to remember to listen—to keep their prescriptions in mind. Although science says to do something, is it something the patient can/will actually do? Do your recommendations fit the patient's schedule? Patients aren't just a number. They're human.

Most doctors when most patients walk into their offices can figure out what's wrong. Brianna's issues were more of a guessing game. Brianna would recount her symptoms, and the doctors would guess what bug she had. A sample of her sputum (spit) in a cup usually identified the bug, but the test took at least a month to give a solid diagnosis.

As Brianna's lover and best friend, it was difficult for me not to think long term. From my perspective, every dose of medicine she took, every breathing treatment she did, added time to her life. As humans, we sometimes get lost in prolonging life without thinking about what that life might look like. Many times, I found myself struggling when Brianna didn't take her medicine. Instead of giving her a hard time, or confronting her—sometimes I even thought it was counterproductive and unpleasant—I found different ways to help make her care easier, less of a burden.

Her nebulizers would be magically ready for her while watching a movie; her IVs would be changed out in the middle of the night so she didn't have to wake up. She always slept through the beeping sound anyway, but I know she appreciated it. It became a ritual. Still frustrating, it was a team effort—one less struggle for her to face alone. Her medicines needed to be refrigerated, so I bought a mini-fridge so we could store them close to the bedroom, making it completely reachable from the bedside, never worrying about forgetting to grab them.

We worked to make it fun—the animals even caught on. Bri would sit in a chair in the living room and use her nebulizer. It's where we stored all her nebulizer supplies. The machine was basically an air compressor. We drilled a hole in the end table so she never had to unplug it, but could store it conveniently near the chair she felt most comfortable doing her nebs in. Hemi and Onyx, our cats, caught on to the sound. Then, every time that nebulizer turned on, no matter where they were in the house, or outside, they came running! They knew that sound meant Brianna was sitting in one spot for thirty minutes or so and that they would get her cuddles. Even the kitties knew how to make it easier for Bri to follow the plan. Although nothing could take away the frustration, these little things helped make it easier—reduced what, to her, felt like someone constantly nagging her. At times, she just didn't feel like following the prescribed regimen, so she just gave CF a fist. She was in control.

As the home treatments became more and more difficult, Brianna had to wear an IV bag with a twenty-four-hour drip. Maintaining her sense of humor, she named the IV bag Chuck—because she wanted to chuck it across the room. It worked for her, so she named her other medical supplies. Her oxygen bag became Larry. Her bag of medicine was Molly. These little things made the weight, the burden, lighter and really made life more fun. It made us laugh. It gave us good times.

Hospital visits were often difficult because the nurses would sometimes forget that having a disease like this made you a professional of your own body, and the nurses would find it hard when you instructed them on the quirks of your body, sometimes offending them unintentionally. Often, Bri would have to point out certain ways to address her body's medical access points.

As Brianna struggled to remain in control, this new bug was a new, difficult relationship for everyone—a new monster to manage, all while living life.

During most of this time, we were blessed to have Brianna's father's insurance, which usually covered everything. When we got married and she reached the age when she was no longer accepted under her dad's insurance, we were faced with paying for a new insurance plan. Since I was self-employed, that meant finding our own plan. Thanks to Obamacare, Brianna was able to get insurance. Before that, her pre-existing conditions would have excluded her from most plans, even the most expensive ones. Every year, at enrollment time, we looked for the perfect plan to help pay for her treatments. A few times, her drugs were well over $30,000 a month. Without insurance, she would have no chance to have a life. However, to pay for the insurance, Brianna had to work. She wanted to work, but it was hard to do when you needed to treat your disease ten hours a day.

Naturally, Brianna was driven. She loved to work and apply herself. Like me, she had known what she wanted to do early in life. We were both driven. With her love for animals came a desire to help them. Medical students from UW, who came to listen to her and ask questions, often suggested she become a doctor, but that didn't involve animals. Animals were her passion. Brianna wanted to be a veterinarian.

Chapter 10

A VETERINARIAN AT HEART

Becoming a veterinarian takes time—school, on-site practice, exams, licensing, all before you have your own practice. But for Brianna, there was no better dream than to help animals. She absolutely loved them and they loved her. She could walk up to any animal and they would cling to her. As a kid, she always had animals. She was in 4-H, showing her horses, and on the drill team for the local rodeo. She showed pigs for FFA. She went to WSU with the end goal of being a large animal veterinarian, specializing in horse dentistry.

This goal would be daunting for anyone, and even more daunting for someone with a life expiration date who was fighting CF daily. It required four years of undergraduate study, then four years of veterinary school. Just to be accepted into the school involved maintaining perfect grades, being selected from a group of handpicked applicants, and giving perfect interviews. Once accepted, it was a grueling four years of veterinary school—an overwhelming experience for most with normal health, let alone those living with a disease that, at times, took you out of commission for days.

Brianna didn't care. She was determined. With anything Brianna did, CF was never an issue. CF was like a younger sibling tagging along behind her.

After her fourth year of college, Brianna applied to the veterinary program. She was already extremely involved with the veterinary school, but it wasn't enough. When she wasn't accepted, she didn't let it get in her way; she went right into taking another try and applied again. This meant another year of retaking classes to increase her score, adding another bachelor certificate to the list, and then reapplying.

Again, it wasn't enough. She was defeated. Her dream shattered. Wanting to give it another try, she struggled with the idea of more time being taken away from her life. She wondered if she would even be able to make it through college alive, let alone live long enough to open her own practice. It was difficult. We talked about it a lot. In her mind, CF was controlling her, holding her back.

College can be difficult for a normal student—you miss a day and it is nearly impossible to catch up. Brianna, because of CF, sometimes missed weeks. A day here because she just felt sick, a day there for doctor appointments, or a visit to the hospital to tackle a flare-up. It was hard to maintain her grades. It was nearly impossible to catch up if you missed one day of college classes, let alone missing a week.

Always devoted to extracurricular activities, Brianna also worked at the school's dairy, worked at the USDA doing tick research, and assisted at a local horse dentistry practice. She even went with her brother Justin to Nicaragua to assist with World Vets. She was devoted and determined, but no matter how hard she worked or how involved she was with veterinary programs—regardless of how much of a perfect fit she was—she was not accepted into veterinarian school.

Frustrating fate had a better plan for Brianna. Still, she graduated with a degree in animal science and zoology. She was the first member of her family to complete a four-year degree—and she managed to do it with two majors, not stopping with just one.

About this time, Brianna developed complications with her CF, making it more difficult to treat. As things progressed, her Spokane CF doctor felt it was bigger than CF—that it was possibly a new macrobacterium that had infiltrated her despite her constant battle—a bug that needed special attention from specialized doctors. The closest specialist was in Seattle at the University Research Facility.

After five years in Pullman, trying a third time to get into the veterinary school would mean another year away before starting another four-year program. There just wasn't enough time in Brianna's life for this. The time she did have would be better spent fighting this new bug, applying herself to her other animal endeavors and ideas.

It didn't go too badly, though. Like I said, fate had another plan for her. God needed her in Poulsbo, or at least in Kitsap County, closer to her family.

Soon after making the decision to move back to Poulsbo, Brianna's best friend Brittany introduced her to a veterinarian who had recently graduated from WSU and was starting her own practice in Port Orchard, just thirty minutes from Brianna's parents' place in Poulsbo. She was looking for staff in the office—ideally, staff who shared her love for animals.

Not wasting much time, Brianna reached out. She was a perfect fit! It didn't take long for the two to connect. Dr. Maci Paden ran a mobile veterinary clinic that focused on large animal care, with some small animals. It was perfect for Brianna. In no time, Maci had seen Brianna's potential, her drive, her love for animals, and understood her story.

The practice was originally housed in a small shed that staff shared with Maci's dogs—they called it the dog office. Later, Maci had a clinic building built to her specifications. Brianna was put in charge of the office and really collaborated with Maci in creating the practice. Maci later described Brianna as her business' better half. Maci was the vet and took care of the business side, while Brianna did what she did best, working with people and their animals.

Maci's clients loved Brianna, just like everywhere else. She drew people into the clinic. Always bubbly while answering calls or welcoming patients, she always had the answers, and she always helped patients feel safe and relaxed in the most difficult times— everything a veterinary clinic needed. Many times I visited her at work and was being completely mesmerized by how she talked people through difficult situations. People usually don't call the vet because their dog just sat for the first time. They only call when something goes wrong, or at best, because it's time for an annual checkup and vaccinations. Plus, going to the vet is stressful because it can be a financial strain. But to hear Brianna talk to people, ease their minds, tell them, "A vet is on the way," and help them make big decisions was amazing. Brianna had that confidence with death; she had a heart for animals and no fear in places where so many were terrified. She loved to be the voice for animals. She truly excelled in every bit of her job. People loved to call just to hear her voice, so much so that when she would take a day off, people usually asked, "Where's Bri?"

Once again, fate, or God's work, if you will. I'm not sure Bri, with her CF, could have been a veterinarian. When she assisted Maci in the field, it was physically challenging; the weather wasn't always pleasant, and the days were long, neither of which was compatible with her CF. But to create her own schedule, work in a heated office, interact with people, love on all the furry pets, bring her IV to work, have the on-site nurse flush and clean her port, and at times wander home for a quick break or snack, gave her light and purpose. Although she didn't get accepted to veterinary school, once again, she was conquering the world, pushing every setback to the side, and making it into a great success.

As Brianna advanced, the clinic advanced, and she began to feel her life had meaning. And she got a title. After all the years of trying to become a vet, she got the next best thing. She became Brianna Strand, Practice Manager. She defined new positions, hired new employees, helped manage the gear, ordered supplies—everything it takes to hold a practice together. She was the nucleus. As practice manager, she was the voice of reason with customers when something didn't go well; she was the HR department for employees, someone to voice their frustrations to; she was the scheduler keeping all the balls (vets) in the air (going where they needed to be), the manager to keep the ship and all its parts floating, and even better, she was everyone's favorite person.

I mean everyone's!

One of Brianna's favorite things was being responsible for the team's retreats. Taking the entire team from the clinic and spending a day together, helping the team build their bonds, grow tighter, and develop as a team all made the clinic better. Designing an entire day's workshop to facilitate such teamwork made Brianna happy. She was a natural at it. During her time as Washington State FFA officer, that was all she did; so now she was just reapplying those skills to the clinic.

But Brianna didn't stop there. She gave every employee the Myers-Briggs personality test assessment to help understand how they interacted. She started a preceptor program through WSU at the clinic. Applicants from all over the world signed up to learn at Clover Valley Vet. If that wasn't enough, she also created VetTalks. This was a free Q&A session offered to the public where the clinic hosts a discussion and gives a presentation on animal health topics, answering all kinds of questions and providing information to the community. The very first session was filled to capacity. There wasn't enough room for everyone who showed up.

After about a year at her parents' house, in 2012, we moved into a rental Maci owned on the clinic's property. It allowed Brianna to drive less and get more sleep, and it allowed us to spend more time together when I was home. I gave her space as much as I could when I was home, but there was nothing more exciting than bringing her lunch and eating together. I also got to help her with tech issues, designing the clinic's network, creating flyers, planning group retreats, and taking pictures for the clinic. Since I wasn't always able to get Brianna's mind off the clinic, it allowed us to spend days together. Waiting anxiously for the invite to visit her at work was hard, but seeing her love her job, and helping her succeed at it, inspired me and fed my fire for her.

Brianna loved her job so much that when she got sick, she sometimes chose to work for animals, instead of staying at home, always bringing her CF with her. When things were getting really bad, one day her mom and sister-in-law came to visit her at work and found her pale and lethargic. They were worried about her condition and convinced her to walk away from work. They dragged her to the CF clinic with a 104 temperature, her bug fully on takeover mode, her body in full attack mode—of course, Brianna had just been continuing on with life. No one at the clinic had even noticed. Often, I or family had to convince her to throw up the white flag, put life aside, and address her CF.

Luckily, Brianna's relationship with Maci and the clinic created a huge support group for her. The staff would attend her yearly walkathon, with Clover Valley Vet becoming one of the event's main sponsors.

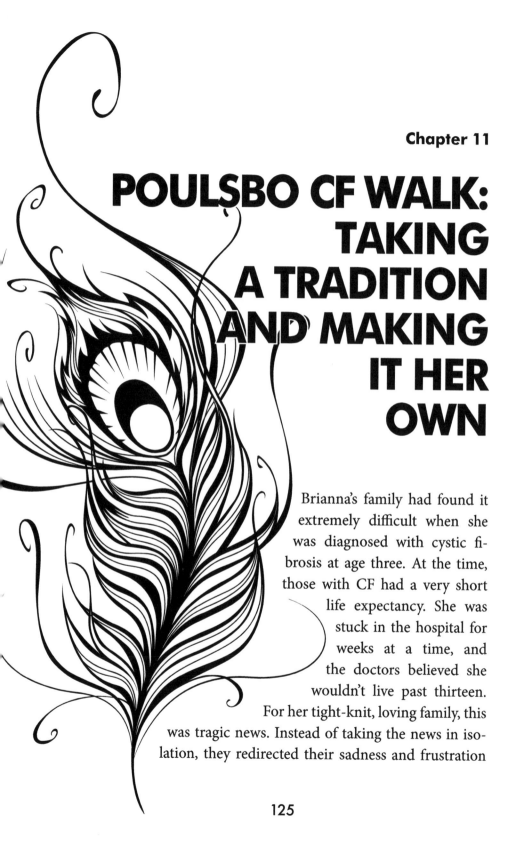

Chapter 11

POULSBO CF WALK: TAKING A TRADITION AND MAKING IT HER OWN

Brianna's family had found it extremely difficult when she was diagnosed with cystic fibrosis at age three. At the time, those with CF had a very short life expectancy. She was stuck in the hospital for weeks at a time, and the doctors believed she wouldn't live past thirteen. For her tight-knit, loving family, this was tragic news. Instead of taking the news in isolation, they redirected their sadness and frustration into fundraising and positive efforts to spread awareness of cystic fibrosis.

Being involved with CF fundraising provided an avenue for them to talk with other families going through the same struggle, people who really understood life with CF. Not long after Brianna was diagnosed, in 1992, the family started a Great Strides walkathon with the Cystic Fibrosis Foundation in Poulsbo. It was one of the first Great Strides Walks to take shape in the state of Washington.

Every year, her family would come together, ask for donations, build hype, invite the community out, and walk through the city, raising money to fight cystic fibrosis. It became a staple community event and was very popular. Brianna's mom and dad always led the effort, taking responsibility for organizing the event. As Brianna grew, one of her dreams was to take over organizing the walkathon. After college, she was able to do so. And, of course, I was excited to help.

Her parents officially stepped aside, and Brianna and I teamed up, giving the walk a whole new energy. The walk had lost some momentum over the twenty-plus years her parents had organized it, as ongoing charity events are prone to do, so taking it on as fresh blood meant finding new ways to make it bigger and attract new faces.

When Brianna asked me to help, I couldn't have been more excited. Like always, I gave Brianna my all and went to work. As a production manager at heart, and now a video wall engineer, this task was second nature for me. I love setting up events because I'm a complex thinker. Staying on top of all the many details, keeping everything organized, solving problems before they happen, and planning a huge event can be stressful, but I crave the challenge.

It was a perfect match. Brianna was the voice, the image, and she did that so well! Her following was like when the title character in the movie *Forrest Gump* ran across the country. Whatever Brianna did, people just kept coming and coming. I worked on everything behind the scenes: planning, scheduling, marketing, advertising, sponsorship. Before we knew it, the whole city was there.

We started out with a new approach, a different way to look at things. One of the biggest goals for us was creating attention. Yes, the fundamental goal was to raise money and awareness. However, we felt by taking the focus off of monetary donations—in a sense, begging for money—and redirecting the focus onto bringing families to the event, creating fun activities for them, and leaving them with a desire to share their experiences and bring more people with them next year, the message would do the work for us. Of course, during the entire event we would share stories and display information, spreading awareness about CF. Brianna would share her story and inspire others to do the same. Before you knew it, record numbers of people were donating, wanting to be part of the cause. It became infectious.

We started by giving the walk a brand. Everyone called it the Poulsbo CF Walk, but all the foundation's advertisements were nationally branded, which didn't help give the local area ownership, or feel a personal connection. We connected with a local graphic designer to create a fun logo. The logo allowed us to create cost-effective, but vibrant and attention-getting mascots. We used green, since it was Brianna's favorite color—and yes, like Brianna said, it was the color of sputum or the bugs Brianna and CFers would cough up. We used purple because it was the national official color for CF. We also used orange and yellow because the foundation was using them in their branding effort at the time.

The new Poulsbo CF walk logo had four people walking as a group, and because Poulsbo had a strong Norwegian heritage, each person wore a set of horns—Viking style. That made it simple to bring it alive, along with spandex costumes, which were donated and also easy to replace. Then we added Poulsbo CF Walk in block lettering. This allowed us to play with words to suit the need. We could make a line that said "Poulsbo CF Walk," or make it a box and have "Poulsbo" on top of "CF Walk." This logo was extremely flexible for branding purposes and made it come to life. Now it was Poulsbo's own.

Next, we needed to get the word out. Ted Sadtler from the Mattress Ranch, a fun mattress company headquartered locally, met with Brianna and was mesmerized. He had invested his support in a prior CF family, but he was conflicted by the sadness hanging over the entire family and lost a form of hope. Brianna and her light changed that. An instant fan, like many, he offered commercials the month prior to the walk, which were broadcast throughout the local area. In Mattress Ranch's commercial style, he allowed us to fully advertise the walk. This was huge. Ted was the founder and a local legend for his silly outfits and farm-style mattress stores. His participation was huge for building momentum.

In addition, we worked on pepping up the event. Before, it was simply the walk, nothing more. People waited around before and after. To help give them something to do, we invited a local monster truck company to display some of its trucks. The fire department, police, Coast Guard, and even the local US Navy and US Army posts brought vehicles to display. The local antique car clubs also joined in.

Some photographers showed up and captured the event. A local photo booth company brought its machine. People had fun taking silly shots in the booth and went home with branded magnets advertising the event on their refrigerators. Local support helped us secure prime advertisement locations where eight by four-foot sheets of plywood were deployed, completely handpainted with our branding advertising the walk. The signs were painted via a huge, donated stencil, creating an easy way to replicate them when needed. The local sign company donated a banner to hang over the city's main street.

As if that were not enough, we began to walk in the city's largest parade, which was conveniently scheduled for two weeks before our event. We walked with our banner and supporters; some rode in classic cars and mini-monster trucks; and, of course, we featured our new, highly anticipated, eye-catching mascots. They were a hit and have become a staple in the city. We were growing hype.

I spent all year planning the event, and sometimes…well, often… annoying the family with my excitement and new plans. Yet I felt good filling up Brianna's smile, devoting energy toward helping her spread awareness, and in the end, reaching her main goal— making CF Stand for Cure Found.

Brianna's family called its team Bri's Believers. The first year Bri was back from college, her college friends attended the event wearing shirts that coined the term BriLievers. Indeed, Brianna made everyone a BriLiever.

Things expanded so quickly that we outgrew our location at the local elementary school. In our first year organizing the event, we went from raising just under $20,000 the year prior to raising more than $50,000.

We were a dream team. Brianna made people believe. She truly did! Speaking to the public, being a voice for so many, she was in her element and naturally beautiful. People flocked to her.

Meanwhile, I took my expertise and polished the event and branding, helping the event to succeed. This was a dream.

Our event grew so quickly that the CF Foundation called to ask us about how we grew our success, and the mayor worked with us to find a new location to accommodate the new growth.

My motivation was Brianna. I truly lived to see her smile. That was my fuel. My desire. It truly made my heart swell! I often said my heart was in the shape of her. It was. It is. And to see her in front of a crowd, everyone mesmerized by her existence, was truly BriMazing.

Chapter 12

PARADISE: STRAND FAMILY FARM

Working at the veterinary clinic was amazing for Brianna. Renting a place next to where she worked was also beneficial, but it was a small place—only 700 square feet. And it didn't have a finished pasture for Dolce. We wanted a place of our own: a farm.

I had tried to save and save, but with the trips we had been making, the cost of medical expenses, the time spent staying home for my mom, and just simply living, saving was difficult. We were trying to wait for the perfect time, but again, we realized there is never a perfect time. If you wait long enough, that time will be gone.

Soon after Mom passed, my uncle passed. My mom was her brother's best friend and his power of attorney. He looked up to my mom. My uncle had had a cancerous brain tumor removed in 1994, and again in 2000, and then the cancer returned just before my mom was diagnosed in 2012. My mom had been helping him through his battle until she was diagnosed, which made things difficult. When my uncle lost his battle with cancer, it was a hard time for the family, with two deaths in just six months.

However, my uncle left some money behind, which helped, and I also got the financial support I needed to finally put some money down on a house.

Brianna and I looked around Port Orchard, where the clinic was located. It was about a half hour drive from Brianna's family and an hour from mine. Port Orchard was a perfect spot. We enlisted Brianna's best friend's mom to be our realtor.

We wanted acreage, a livable space, and a second space to rent out for some possible added income. The first couple of places we looked at needed work—lots of work.

The third place we looked at was something special. I didn't realize it at first, shooting it down when I saw it on paper. But we went to see it anyway. When we pulled up, Brianna lit up. Her smile told me it would take a lot of work to convince her this wasn't the place for us.

First, the street was a private gravel road named Cozy Lane. The place was the second on your right—just far enough to be off the main street but close enough that you didn't have to drive too far.

As you entered, to the right you looked over to see a full three acres of pasture, open land, with a natural stream going through the middle. As you turned into the driveway, you pulled up to a gate with a huge archway. As you continued to pull in, you drove around a set of evergreen trees that completely hid the house from the street. On the other side, as you pulled in, you sat at the top of a hill overlooking the three-acre pasture and completely displaying the entire field. Pulling up to the house, you entered a circular drive with trees in the middle. The house was beautiful, nestled into the countryside. As we parked, I looked over, and without even talking, could tell Brianna was already home. She knew before she even opened the front door.

Finally, Brianna spoke through that smile of hers. "This is the place. Let's make an offer." I had to laugh. We hadn't even seen the place yet. I was nervous. Plus, before making this kind of big purchase, you always sleep on it. Not Brianna.

We got out to look inside, for my sake, I guess. From the sell sheet, you could tell the place needed some work. It was a foreclosure, so it was a bit in our favor, financially. The pasture needed new fencing. All the field fence was weighed down by many years of animals kicking up dirt and pushing it down. It definitely needed work, but it was perfect. We could personalize it and make it our own.

It had a small water shed where the pump was located, a small barn with a little storage for tack and some extra hay, and a huge outbuilding used for hay storage. Everything was perfectly placed and had character.

When we finished looking around the outside, it was time to look inside. Inside, we were welcomed with missing floors and a staircase with no railing. A couple of sticks held caution tape. This was definitely something we would have to address right away if we were going to purchase it. Walking in farther, we saw a post in the middle of the room, covered by a tree someone had hollowed out and placed around it. It was beautiful, made to look like a tree was going through the house. Beyond that was the living room. It had full, 180-degree-view windows, looking out into the backyard, which was full of evergreens and a beautiful salmon stream. There was a brick wall with an old-style, standout fireplace. It was one of those old rustic pieces that reach out from the brick wall. Wood floors all around the upstairs finished off the look. That was what we had walked into—3,000 square feet of beautiful. Two bedrooms and two bathrooms upstairs, and a complete downstairs with an additional bedroom, living space, storage area, and laundry room. It had room for growth—so we could add character and personalize it—and more importantly, it was in good enough shape that we could move in right away.

At this point, Brianna was sold. It would have been near-impossible to talk Brianna out of buying this house at that point. But really, as we walked around, we both shared ideas for personalizing it, for making it our own. It was kind of like playing house as kids.

Before we even left, we were ready to make an offer. The first offer, which was somewhat less than we had planned to spend, was accepted.

During the couple of months it took to get into the house, I made many trips there, planning the electric gate, security cameras, garage door openers, speakers, and fence line, and cleaning the roof and gutters—things that helped make it easier for Brianna. We were so excited.

Right after we moved in, I started on the fence line for Dolce. I hired a tractor to help with the 200-plus fence posts, using the tractor to dig all the holes, while I shoveled and tamped damp gravel into each and every one by hand. It was a lot of work, but a very rewarding project. We used a three-line horse fence, called Equi-Fence, so once the vertical posts were up, the rest went up with ease. It was hard to keep Brianna from working too hard outside, so most of the time, I worked while she was at work. Since installing the line was easy, we were able to finish it together. Before you knew it, three weeks had gone by, and we were ready for Dolce to finally come home.

With Bentley, Onyx, Hemi, Dorito the hedgehog, and our tortoise Burger, our funny farm was well on its way. The Strand Family Farm truly was turning into a paradise. One of our favorite things to do was sit outside in the grass overlooking the pasture. Usually, when we did this, Dolce would come running from wherever she was to break up our alone time. She loved being snuggled. To sit in a pasture and watch Dolce trot up was so peaceful and fulfilled one of Brianna's true dreams, giving us a feeling like we lived in the wild and in a state of bliss.

Bentley and the cats were always close by, never leaving our sides. Walking around the farm was like being in a parade, with all the animals trying to get involved in everything. This place was everything Brianna could have dreamed of, plus more. And with her smiles, her excitement, and her dreams coming true, my heart was swollen with love—and my dream of making her world of dreams a reality came true.

As things progressed, to help Brianna be more independent, I kept making modifications to the place. She absolutely loved feeding the animals, morning and night. And she had to do it. It was part of being independent. The hay barn was located away from the smaller barn, so when the hay bales ran out, moving them over was tough. Usually, she had to enlist her dad to come move some over when I wasn't home. It was a struggle mentally for Brianna. To help, we purchased a tractor and put the hay in the hay barn on pallets, ripping open the side and installing a new door where we kept the hay. When it ran out, all Brianna had to do was hop on the John Deere, scoop up a palate, and replenish the hay for the animals.

The daily exercise of feeding all her animals helped Brianna stay strong and healthy—as much as she could considering the fight always going on within her body. It also provided for some great Bentley and Brianna fetch time. Having a wide open, five-acre plot of land provided such a great life for the cats and dog. It was great just to open a door and let the animals venture out. As the protector, Bentley would morning and night make his rounds, as we called it. After doing his business, he would walk the line smelling all the smells.

Having all these animals was a doctor's nightmare with all the germs and bacteria associated with them, but Brianna required her livelihood, and animals were a huge part of her happy place.

Early in our relationship, Brianna and I had made a pact to get rid of cable, so nights at home were often about cuddling up on the couch and watching a movie. *Cars*, *Monsters, Inc.*, and *Finding Nemo* were among our favorites. At the same time, we often just sat and enjoyed the silence. Siting on the other side of the couch, I would massage her feet, eventually transitioning into her massaging mine. Our talks were simple, never forced, but always continuous. They ran the gamut from things that happened at work, to things going on with the walk, to talks about CF, and sometimes, death.

It was rare Brianna was able to sleep comfortably. As things got worse, she often sat up, resting against a pile of pillows to keep her airways clear so she could try to get some sleep. She was often jarred awake by coughing fits. I didn't sleep well, either. If it wasn't coughing waking me up, it was the sound of her late-night munching on a bag chips. She was constantly eating to fuel her body, trying to replace the energy being expended by the inner struggle.

Brianna's inspiration defined the house. Western decor was everywhere; a collage of canvas prints covered the stairwell walls; her grandparents' bear rug was hung up; a decal announced you were at "Strand Family Farm," and, of course, there were her quotes—the fridge was covered not with magnets, but with quotes she had written with different colored markers, then cut out, arranged, and taped to the fridge as a constant reminder each time you were in the kitchen. Some of the quotes were:

"Laugh as much as you breathe; love as much as you live." — Johnny Depp

"Common sense isn't common." — Anonymous

"She who laughs last didn't get it." — Carroll Bryant

"We are what we repeatedly do. Excellence, therefore, is not an act, but a habit." — Aristotle

"Never argue with a fool; people might not know the difference." — Mark Twain

"Well-behaved women seldom make history." — Laurel

Thatcher Ulrich

A 3,000 square-foot house wasn't what we had desired, but it went with the property. We barely used the downstairs because of its size and the fact that a couple of trips up and down tired Brianna out. The empty space provided some great opportunities and memories, though.

One of the best times was when her brother Justin and his family used the downstairs space for a whole year. In 2016, two years after we moved in, Brianna flew to Austin to drive back with her brother in a U-Haul with all their stuff, as his family drove ahead. Justin and Brianna used a paper map instead of Google as a way to make the trip more fun and entertaining. Brianna had them stop to explore all the fun things along the way. Her and her quirky adventures—she made her brother go see the world's largest hairball, and many more "fun" roadside attractions. Their week-long adventure helped the two of them catch up after Brianna had been off to school and Justin had been in Texas. With the empty space in the house, we had the opportunity to play host for a full year and really get to know Justin's family, consisting of him, his wife Erica, and their son, Jack, who was almost three.

Nothing was more exciting than hearing Jack scream to Brianna from downstairs, "Auntie Bri!"

"Hi, Jack!" she would reply.

"Hi, Auntie Bri!" Jack would yell, and then he would rush upstairs to break into Brianna's always full snack drawer—fruit snacks, Rice Krispies treats, chocolates, and any other crazy candies she craved. The nieces and nephews usually made a mad dash for the drawer whenever they visited. Brianna purposely kept it at reachable height for them.

Brianna made daily visits downstairs, and I would follow. Jack would play with his toys, while Brianna, Justin, and his wife Erica would drink coffee and just chat about life and bond like they did so well. At one point, I noticed that Justin and Brianna shared a family trait of both making a random noise in their throats—something completely random, yet unique between the two.

Our paradise truly created beautiful memories. This book's cover, which features her amazing beauty, is not a picture from our actual wedding. With so much going on at the wedding, we somehow missed some of the main pictures Brianna wanted to capture on our wedding day. We wanted a shot of Brianna in her dress in the pasture with her horse. Thankfully, Brianna and her dad were able to make it happen after the fact. Her mom and her niece Rylee helped with makeup, hair, and getting her wedding dress out. Brianna then ventured out to the pasture, joining her dad with the camera, who captured the cover picture.

Her beauty was what drew most people's attention. But her power was visible, politely letting her beauty take center stage. What you don't see was her 101-degree temperature, or her removing the needle and setting her IV aside so she could jump into her wedding dress and let her beauty radiate. Yet she did it with ease, without any sign that she was in a constant war to keep her body alive.

Chapter 13

LIFE OF A ROADIE

My and Brianna's relationship was growing. So were our careers. Being a roadie brought me challenges but also many great opportunities. With most tours, I was away for less than four weeks—six at the most. Then I would have a week at home before going back out. If the tour was finished, it meant being home 24/7.

Being in a long-distance relationship is difficult. It takes a special someone. But it was also extremely beneficial. When you're apart much of the time, you have to communicate—express love through words—and support each other. Removing the physical presence of visual expressions makes you love through words and communication.

By texting all day with a few calls thrown in, we were never disconnected. We would talk before bed, sharing the status of our minds. We were excited to share stories, and anxious to talk through life's challenges, sharing pictures of each other being silly, making silly faces, or of our expeditions that day. On FaceTime, I watched Brianna fight for the screen as all the animals devoured her with attention, sometimes…often…knocking the propped-up phone over. Even the animals missed me.

It wouldn't take long before I would be home. When I was home, I had no work obligations. Home meant me time. Us time. Brianna time. We were inseparable. Work was an ever-changing schedule, making it hard to plan around. But we created a system that worked. Brianna would just plan, and I would hop on the train and join her for whatever she had planned. In my eyes, being with her was all I needed. It didn't matter what we were doing as long as we were together. When she was at work was about the only time we weren't together. But even then, I usually stopped by for lunch and often hung around to help with whatever project she was working on. I helped with technical issues, designing flyers, taking her meds, or just keeping her company.

Always being together, then being apart while I was on the road gave us an advantage, strengthened our communication, and kept us from taking each other for granted.

We never said goodbye; it was always a "See you soon!" One of our ways to express ourselves was to share songs expressing our feelings. A few songs really spoke to our true feelings. Journey's song "Faithfully" came the closest. Like the song says, it was hard being apart, but every time Brianna picked me up at the airport, giddily jumping for joy as she ran to give me a hug that had been brewing for weeks, I knew there was no better joy in my life.

We would send songs like "I Feel Home" by O.A.R., or more importantly, "You & Me" by Dave Matthews Band to each other and listen while on the phone together. One of the bigger songs was definitely "You & Me." We were a dream team. It felt amazing. And like the man said, she and I could do anything together.

Working shows made for wonderful times bringing Brianna out on the road to visit. We often saw the shows I worked, getting intimate, behind-the-scenes looks at the bands. We watched Rush rehearsals on the 2007 Snakes and Arrows tour, provided many first-row experiences with her and her friends on tours I was on like Tim McGraw 2010 Southern Voice Tour and Maroon 5 2010 Hands All Over Tour.

Once the family went to see Stevie Wonder in Seattle on the 2014 Songs of the Key of Life Performance Tour, and a little after getting to the seats, her dad struck up a conversation with the people sitting next to them. It turned out they were sitting next to Pearl Jam's lead singer, Eddie Vetter. Jim, Brianna's dad, being a guitarist, became awestruck later realizing this.

Another time, Brianna came backstage to see me on the 2016 Sting and Peter Gabriel Rock, Paper, Scissors tour. She bumped into Sting, getting a quick introduction and a handshake.

However, the artist encounter that stood out the most was when I toured with Kelly Clarkson. Doing two tours with her gave me almost two full years of work—and it gave Brianna some great experiences. One night on the 2012 Stronger Tour, the band was playing Universal Studios in Orlando, Florida. I had a few days off, which I flew Brianna in for. We saw the show, and then I got a VIP pass from management to enjoy the amusement park. We got to go to the front of the line to see the Harry Potter Adventure, a dream of Brianna's. Random miracles like that often occur on the road.

The Stronger 2012 tour ended randomly in Pullman, blocks away from where we lived at the time. Rylee, Brianna's niece, was a huge fan of Kelly's, so when we got tickets for the whole family to see her, Brianna became Super-Aunt. We brought Rylee backstage to meet Kelly prior to the show, and then during the show, the whole family sang every song at the top of their lungs, while they visited me at work. This was a little girl's dream experience, and it made Auntie Bri glow! To this day, Rylee still displays the personally signed poster on her wall with the picture of the family and Kelly.

When I was home, we had plenty of time to do fun things. Brianna was a huge Seahawks fan, so if a game was on, we would be watching it with her family, as she screamed at the TV. My dad and brother had bought season tickets to the Seahawks since the stadium opened in 2012, so on occasion, they gifted us the tickets. Brianna loved going to the games.

Somehow, up to this point, being home aligned perfectly with Brianna's doctor visits, and usually if I had to miss an appointment, her mom and/or dad went with her. At least one of the three of us was always there with her for support.

Brianna understood my love for my work, my career on the road, and my role behind the scenes with music. She understood it so much that she often convinced me to go to work over my extreme desire to be present for her during medical visits. Luckily, there weren't many conflicts. However, as doctor visits became more frequent, and the abscessus became more present, juggling medical visits and work became an issue.

In early February 2017, after almost thirty-one solid months of twenty-four-hour IVs and two solid cultures not growing any abscessus, the doctors were confident enough to tackle her CF head on. As a doctor, part of science is a guessing game. But with a new drug on the market, Orkambi, that showed positive results in directly attacking the root cause of her form of CF, both the infectious disease team and her CF team were ready to go to war. If it worked, it meant slowing down the progression of her CF and the abscessus, her lungs regaining function, and raising her pulmonary function test scores, and possibly extending her life.

At this point, Brianna's lung function had dropped dramatically. When we first met in 2007, it was 85 percent. As the bug abscessus started to show its ugly head in 2010, she dropped to 56 percent in a matter of weeks, which signaled her Spokane team to send over to Dr. Pottinger at the University of Washington. The bug was under control until it randomly popped up again in 2015, plunging her lung function from 45 percent down to only 25 percent. At that point, I fought her to get her to use oxygen. She didn't need it, but it helped. I finally convinced her to at least wear it around the house and while sleeping.

Wearing oxygen felt great because it helped her not labor so much to breathe and let her body work less hard to replenish oxygen. But it meant giving up some of her independence to CF. Brianna didn't like that. She also didn't want to explain the oxygen to people if she had to wear it every day.

As the months passed—twelve months, twenty-four months, finally thirty-one months of treatment—her lungs remained at 25 percent and showed two solid months of abscessus-free sputum samples. Because she had been solidly stable for a couple of years, and with clear sputum samples, the doctors felt Brianna's body was ready. The abscessus was suppressed enough to be dormant. This meant they could try taking her off her IVs and try the new Orkambi. As Orkambi was new, she had to completely be off everything else to find a baseline, so when she started taking it, the doctors could monitor her improvement—or, in the worst-case scenario, her decline.

This change was exciting. It meant possibly getting the upper hand. With so much confidence, and feeling high from taking such a huge step, Brianna was determined to try to have a child. At the same time, I had just confirmed a three-month tour overseas, starting at the end of March, taking me through Europe, Australia, and New Zealand. It was another perfect opportunity to fly Brianna out for a whole new adventure.

As we attended our final appointment to confirm and make the transition, to break her thirty-one-month relationship with Chuck, her clingy IV bag, and start her new relationship popping Mr. Orkambi, Brianna was determined to, instead of just settling for a home run, go for the gold. She was excited to take a leap.

We asked Dr. Dandekar, because he was the CF doctor directly prescribing the Orkambi, if she was fit to travel to Australia while I was there, and then we asked the gut-wrenching question, "Is it safe to try for a child?" We often forget doctors feel the emotions involved in our situations. After all, they are human. Dr. Dandekar understood how much a child would mean to Brianna, but he also explained how the pregnancy would undermine her body. Sinking into his seat, defeated, he crushed Brianna's hopes with the facts. A high-risk pregnancy required 50 percent lung function or higher. At 25 percent, it was nearly impossible. With these facts, Dr. Dandekar was very much against the idea of Brianna getting pregnant, for good reason.

Then grasping for some good news to deliver, Dr. Dandekar gave his blessings for Brianna to travel to Australia.

They both looked so defeated, sunk into their chairs, holding back their emotions; neither would shed a tear.

Brianna was crushed, and so was Dr. Dandekar.

It caused Brianna to understand how sick she really was, and what it all really meant. I often wondered whether this was another way to indirectly check her status and the disease's severity and progression. But heck, we both dreamed of having a kid.

As Brianna received this defeating news from her CF team, Dr. Pottinger was waiting on the other side of the clinic, in the infectious disease office, working on something as yet unknown to her.

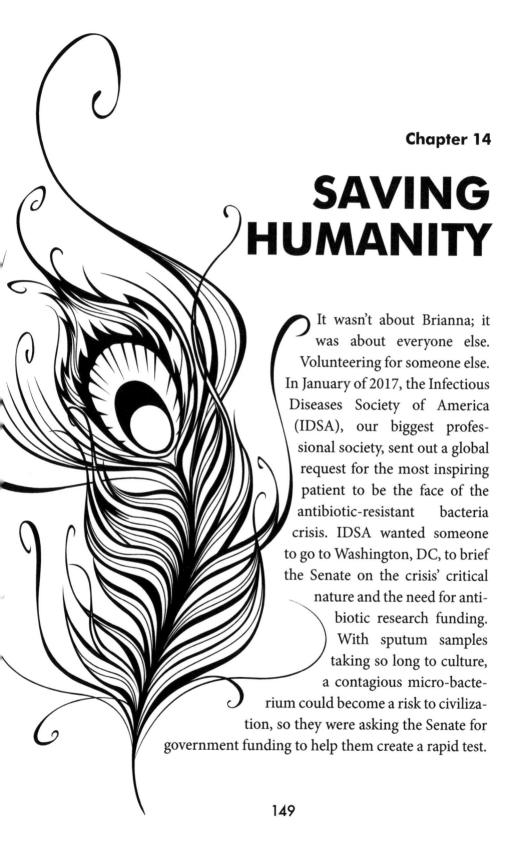

Chapter 14

SAVING HUMANITY

It wasn't about Brianna; it was about everyone else. Volunteering for someone else. In January of 2017, the Infectious Diseases Society of America (IDSA), our biggest professional society, sent out a global request for the most inspiring patient to be the face of the antibiotic-resistant bacteria crisis. IDSA wanted someone to go to Washington, DC, to brief the Senate on the crisis' critical nature and the need for antibiotic research funding. With sputum samples taking so long to culture, a contagious micro-bacterium could become a risk to civilization, so they were asking the Senate for government funding to help them create a rapid test.

149

I always got excited for Brianna. It wasn't a thing I did just to make her feel good. I honestly, genuinely got excited. Even for the little things. She called me many times just to tell me something simple because she knew I would get genuinely excited every time.

In Brianna's case, the micro-bacteria were not an immediate danger. In CF situations where the definitive test takes a long time, doctors test, but more so guess, comparing symptoms to past diagnoses. Then they prescribe certain drugs, hoping one will slow down or stop whatever macrobacteria is attacking.

A rapid test would allow for almost instant identification of the bug, making it much easier for the team to identify a clear and appropriate response. But to get funding, they needed a patient who would benefit from the new test—a human face for the Senate and those voting to associate with the idea. Someone who let them see firsthand how, or whom, financial support would help.

Dr. Pottinger sent in Brianna's name without a second thought. IDSA responded by wanting to interview her. They emailed Brianna, telling her she was selected to be interviewed.

Brianna was shocked and excited, but, like always, she didn't give it a second thought. She came to me with that face, the face where she tried to hold back the excitement, but where you could also see her humbleness. She was so good at double expressions!

When I read the email, I couldn't resist—I instantly responded with joy, telling her she had to do it. I said, "Yeah, no big deal. They just want you to come in and, basically, save the world." Her humbleness, of course, overshadowed my enthusiasm. Reaffirming my statement, I told her, "They want you to help get funding for a rapid test for antibiotic resistance research. Basically, this test, if funded, would help prevent huge catastrophes, save lives, and really, save the world." Yes, my statement was a little overdone, but true.

It was like in the movies when the government needs your specialty and experience for something coming up in the White House. Like in *Independence Day* when the alien researchers finally matter, or like in *Transformers* when the researcher has all the secret information. That was Brianna. We laughed about the secret service randomly dropping by, taking her to save the world.

This was exciting, so there was no way I was going to miss it—or let her miss it. Like always, I did what I could to make sure Brianna's family was involved. I knew how much family meant to her and me, really. I knew how much Brianna meant to her family. I also knew, not clearly, how important it was to take advantage of these situations. When we asked them, her brother Justin and mom Val planned to go. We scheduled the trip, booked adjoining hotel rooms, and planned to extend our stay to take full advantage of this trip.

It was extremely exciting, but it was also going to take a lot of work. At the time, Brianna's lung function had dropped to 25 percent. She seemed to handle it fine, but she got winded more easily and was still resisting constant oxygen; however, she always kept oxygen with her.

We needed to bring her nebulizer, oxygen, all her medications, and doctor's letters for the airline so there would be no issues going through security and boarding the flights. It was a five-hour flight. That's a long time in the air, especially for someone who needs resources like oxygen, so we had to prepare and make sure we had enough for the entire trip.

Then it was time to work on Brianna's speech. She was always nervous about public speaking, but she had an amazing knack for it. I always saw her nervousness as a way for her to downplay her genius. It didn't take long to write the speech, so in a couple of days, she was ready.

We were excited to travel, but there was also some stress. Okay, a lot of stress. Brianna wasn't feeling well. It was getting to her, unlike normal. Her breathing was more difficult. Her attitude seemed affected. No acute symptoms, but you could sense something was taking her strength. The surest identifier was that she felt it herself, and expressed it.

As Brianna's spouse, it was hard mentally and physically to see her feeling bad. She was my number one. I was all about taking care of her, thinking ahead about potential issues so she wouldn't have to, preparing her meds, changing anything to make things easier so she didn't waste any of her energy, and just snuggling with her when she needed warmth.

But I think I needed her more than she needed me. Life was easier when it was just the two of us. With her family, it was a different story. I wanted them there; their presence was very important to me and more so to Brianna. But to be totally honest, it was hard to share Brianna's time. I ended up feeling like an assistant. I did the planning and work and then seemed stuck in the background.

The first day in DC, Brianna met with US Senator Patty Murray to talk about funding at the state level. In the main lobby of the Hart State Senate Building in Washington, DC, the IDSA representative came to meet Brianna and walk her into the meeting. We watched them walk away as they went behind closed doors where she attended state meetings with US Senator from Washington, Patty Murry.

Brianna naturally seemed strong; she spoke clearly, stood tall, and, of course, her smile was radiant, with *the glow of power*. The only sign of strain you might notice, and only if you saw her regularly, was her slight weight loss from her body fighting using every resource it had. Otherwise, there was no indication of the war inside her body.

The day was fast-paced, but Brianna did all she could to keep up. Still, it was wearing on her. Inside, her body was fighting at a whole other level.

After the meetings, we went back to the hotel, where Brianna rehearsed her speech in front of us, over and over, with nebulizer in hand and the oxygen on.

The next morning was the big day. We slowly got up and made our way to the hill to speak in front of the Senate. This event was huge. Brianna liked to talk it down, maybe so it didn't make her so nervous, but come on—she was saving humanity as we know it.

When we showed up, we received the itinerary. Brianna's time was tucked into the middle between the country's leading infectious disease experts and advocates.

Brianna's brother Justin, Mom Val, and I were guided to the audience of chairs, while she was taken to the front with the rest of the speakers. Brianna was sitting with a group of people that featured every single major player in the fight against infectious disease.

When her time came, Brianna looked as beautiful as always and so professional. She walked up to the lectern with her superhuman strength, full of confidence, and began to speak:

Hello and good afternoon. I am Brianna Strand, and I am so honored to be here today to share my story and advocate for the many patients and families who have been and still are affected by multi-drug resistant bacteria. I'd like to share a little about myself. I am twenty-eight years old, married to my best friend, have an incredible family, am a huge Seahawks fan, and am an animal lover. I live on a small farm in Port Orchard, Washington, where I get to spend time with my horses, mini-cows, mini-pig, dogs, cats, and even a tortoise.

I was diagnosed at three years old with cystic fibrosis, or CF, a genetic, progressive disease that causes difficulty breathing and persistent lung infections. It occurs because of a gene mutation that causes a thick, sticky mucus to build up in the lungs, the pancreas, and other organs in the body—this mucus becomes very difficult to get rid of; it is the perfect spot for bacteria to thrive and cause infection. Currently, CF has no cure. To try to prevent infections and keep my lungs healthy, I use multiple nebulizers and inhalers, oral antibiotics, digestive enzymes, and respiratory therapy—I spend an average of two to three hours per day doing my CF therapy.

When I was younger, CF mainly affected my sinuses, so my lung function remained higher, and I bounced back from infections more quickly. It wasn't until my early twenties that my lungs came more into the picture, and my infections required longer treatments of IV antibiotics. In my junior year of college, my CF doctor recommended I be seen by an infectious disease, or ID, department at the University of Washington because he felt my decline in weight and lung function might be due to a different bacteria they would be able to diagnose. So, when I finished school, my husband and I moved back to western Washington, and I transferred all of my care to the university.

It was then I first met the incredible Dr. Pottinger and his team in the ID department at UW. A sputum sample confirmed I did have mycobacterium abscessus, and like many multi-drug resistant bacteria, it can be difficult to treat. It requires taking multiple antibiotics for long periods of time. Even then, it is rare to consider the infection gone, and most likely a person will live with it forever. After both my CF and ID teams discussed my case and drug interactions, three new antibiotics were added to my daily routine.

For the next two years, I continued on these antibiotics, treating my ID and CF bacteria. My daily routine had grown slightly in length, but it was manageable.

The year 2014 brought with it a new level of adulthood for myself—when your chronic illness interferes with your job. Having graduated with degrees in animal science and zoology, I was two years into my dream job as the practice manager at a large animal vet clinic. My work required long hours, and I loved it, but I began to get sicker, and soon I was trying to balance my job with an increasing lung infection and the medications needed to treat it. Not surprisingly, after a few days of chills, constant nausea, headaches, and night sweats, I was admitted to the hospital with a 104-degree temperature, and a chest x-ray confirmed pneumonia.

Instead of improving over the next four weeks, I continued to decline and lost a total of twenty pounds. After coughing up a large amount of blood, I was transferred to the ICU at the University of Washington. My doctors decided to completely stop every antibiotic I was on for forty-eight hours to give my body a break—by the third day, I was finally feeling better. A follow-up image of my lungs showed a surprising amount of damage had been done in that period—the antibiotics had stopped working, and the bacteria were thriving.

After my hospital stay, my doctors struggled with what medications to put me on—balancing my current health and my quality of life with more risky medications, and their slew of side effects was not an easy decision, but it was the right decision, and we were able to back off the infection. That magic formula of meds has brought me to the present and it included an IV that infused 24/7—I'd like to take a moment to introduce "Chuck," my IV pump/fanny pack that was my constant companion for the last thirty-one months. He earned his name "Chuck" because I wanted to chuck him across the room.

Naming my IV bag was one way I found to deal with my new "normal." My faith in God keeps my hope alive, the support of my family keeps my spirits up, and my animals keep me active. All of this is important because, even though I've grown up with a lung disease, it is hard to accept these new changes to my daily life. I now need oxygen to sleep and to exercise, and [doing] simple tasks like feeding my horses depletes my energy.

Having CF and now having MDR abscessus has been a blessing in ways I never imagined—the people I get to meet and the opportunities, like this one today, are truly an honor. I have never wished CF away because it's a part of who I am, but my new reality is very different from the one I pictured as a little girl.

Number one, I worked my whole life knowing I wanted to end up in the veterinary field, and I landed a dream job right out of college. I had a great team of employees and a boss who was very understanding, but with all of the medications and the side effects, my body could not handle it any more—it was time to focus solely on my health. It has been seven months since I left my job, and I still miss it every day. Now I am a full-time farm manager, which I do love, and I consider myself a stay-at-home mom to my kid, CF. Much like kids, you have to constantly take care of CF, and it is a part of my life forever. It also takes a village.

Number two, living with a progressive disease, I've grown up knowing I may go to heaven sooner than planned. But really, we're all dying. Now, I can't tell you that my lungs would or would not be in the shape they are in if abscessus was not around, but my reality is I am living every day with 25 percent lung function. At 30 percent, typically you get referred to the lung transplant team. However, my bacteria makes me ineligible because experience has shown doctors that transplanting lungs that have abscessus will kill an individual faster than if they didn't have the surgery. Most individuals never leave the hospital.

My third reality is a very personal one. My husband and I have always planned to have a family of our own, but with the types of medication I am on and the state my lungs are in, that is not a possibility. If you have children of your own or plan to in the future, you can imagine how difficult this one is to accept.

I didn't share my story for you to feel sorry for me or to pity me. We all have hurdles and limitations in life, but it's not about that limitation; it's about the power you give that limitation. My hope is that by sharing my story today, you feel inspired—inspired to get involved with funding research for new medications and inspired to help make a difference for someone affected by these bacteria. Most importantly, I hope you use that inspiration to be a part of something life changing.

Brianna had freaking nailed it. I was so proud of her. How could you not be! She killed it with 25 percent lung function, with the director of the CDC waiting her turn to follow behind Brianna. What an honor.

Just like that, Brianna made history, forever recorded in the Senate minutes of the United States of America.

We made the best of the next couple of days, taking a stroll through the National Zoo, walking through the Smithsonian, and even a private tour through the Capitol Building.

Exhausted from an amazing time, yet winded from the storm brewing inside, on the last day, we cut our adventures short to bring Brianna back to the hotel because her energy was depleted. This was often a sign that her infection was brewing.

We did all we could to get her home in one piece. She was completely exhausted and weak, becoming frailer. We limped to the airport and boarded our flight. At this point, we were just doing what we could to get home.

At home, we geared up to go into the clinic Monday morning first thing because her temperature and her condition were becoming more and more urgent. One hard thing about traveling with a chronic disease, and thereby compromising your immune system, is the high risk of simple viral infections, or the common cold, which can be very difficult to cope with when your body is already fighting infection. Upon arriving, the doctors sent us right up to the hospital to monitor and help her through what seemed to be a viral infection. After a few days in the hospital, we were headed home.

For most, going home from the hospital usually means healing, or at least that you are stable enough to be home. And really, for Brianna, the battle was still raging, but nothing was getting worse. So instead of living in the hospital, it was time to take the condition home, where one can be more comfortable. Home was really Brianna's desired spot.

As we headed home, I could sense the stress of Brianna's condition. But like a train, time was starting to move quicker and quicker—almost too fast to take it all in and process it. Instead, we fought to keep Brianna stable.

She wasn't getting better, and it was time to decide, before it got too late, to hand the walk over to the foundation for the year. If that wasn't hard enough, before we could settle in back home, Dr. Pottinger called to check in on Brianna, but also, to share some bad news. Brianna's abscessus, which she had worked over thirty-one months to subdue, had grown in her last sputum sample. This was a blow not only to Brianna, but to Dr. Pottinger himself. He wanted to be the one to share the tragic news because they were fighting this together.

Brianna's condition wasn't getting any better. Just ten days after getting home, her war was compromising her body. We had to go back to the hospital. With the complications growing and her losing weight, we finally decided to install a feeding tube to help Brianna's body gain nutrients and energy before they were completely absorbed by the battle raging within.

In the hospital, Brianna's will and hope were not at all compromised. Her spirit remained full of hope. To her, like any other hospital visit, this was just another battle that, in her mind, was already won.

But it seemed like she was keeping something from me. We kept ending up back in the hospital, and with work taking me overseas in a few days for a long period, I was sensing things weren't adding up. Every time I brought up going overseas, Brianna bravely tried to convince me to go, reassuring me she was going to be all right—things were going to turn around. But I was feeling, sensing a different reality. I called work to tell them I might not be able to make the tour and to find a replacement to put on standby as I prepared for the worst.

At this point, Brianna was still pushing me to go, but she was still in the hospital. I made my way home to pack and returned for one more night before my flight. When I was gone, her mom took over, never leaving her side, and always making sure someone was with her. It was hard to leave. At the same time, I thought it would be good to rebuild some energy and gain some clarity away from the situation.

Note:
Video of Brianna's speech is available online at
ChooseYourAttitude.org/BriMazing.

Chapter 15

HARDWARE UPGRADE

I was all packed and ready to go overseas. About halfway across Puget Sound, riding on the ferry, on my way to the airport, I tried to compose an Instagram post to commemorate my mom's birthday, March 30. My post turned into a call from Brianna. She usually texted. We talked often, but with me arriving soon, this call must be urgent. It had to be something serious. At this time, Brianna was alone in the hospital. She was rarely left alone, but there was an hour when no one was available.

The phone rang.

I answered….

Instantly, I could tell something was wrong. Brianna

was in tears, barely getting a breath in. I was trying to understand what she was saying. Her doctor had talked to her about the idea of a lung transplant, and he made it sound urgent. None of her doctors had ever talked about a transplant before; she wasn't a good candidate for one. We had talked about it between ourselves, but the doctors had never given it much attention. And honestly, neither did Brianna.

When we talked about it, she was usually against it. With her ideal of quality over quantity, she didn't see the advantage. Her view of lung transplants was simple: You had to wait until your health was bad enough for you to be placed on the list, yet good enough to survive. If you made the list, and found a lung, your odds under the best conditions were pretty dismal, with many not making it through the surgery. If you were lucky enough to make it through the surgery, you woke up inhaling a full extended amount of fresh air. But only if your body accepted the new, foreign lungs and/or if your new lungs accepted your body. And if they did, you spent the rest of your life taking pills to suppress your immune system so your body wouldn't reject the new lungs. In a CF patient, new lungs don't mean no more CF. Nor do they mean any of your bugs are washed away. Your sinuses are just as much of a bacterium, superbug war zone as they were before.

A few times, her sinus doctors had removed marble-sized bacteria from Brianna's sinuses. Having this already infested breeding ground, a new set of lungs, complete with a suppressed and compromised immune system, didn't win you anything. Yes, you could possibly get more time, but the disease was still on the attack. Brianna didn't want to do that. She would rather live the days she had left to the fullest.

The doctors also acknowledged that, with her superbug abscessus, Brianna's chance of survival was dramatically reduced. The procedure itself was so limited for antibiotic-resistant bacteria abscessus patients that only one clinic in the world would even consider performing the transplant. The clinic had had success, but most patients didn't even make it out of the hospital. And these were healthier patients.

With all that in mind, we understood if we were going to attempt a transplant, now was the time. We were confident in our stance, but we had never faced a situation where a transplant was our only option.

There was so much to think about. And yet, here I was on a ferry, with my suitcase packed, planning to fly off for an extended gig overseas. Clearly, I would be canceling the gig as soon as I got off the phone with Brianna. But still she demanded I not do so. My gut knew what I had to do, but Brianna's confidence had me confused. I mean, she was always right, so she must be right now.

Dr. Pottinger had given us his personal number. Out of respect, we had never used this particular lifeline, but now I needed a voice of reason. When Dr. Pottinger answered, I explained my confusion, what my gut was telling me versus what Brianna was telling me, and asked him for clarity. For the first time, I heard Dr. Pottinger's tone change: "Brianna needs you right now more than ever."

When we hung up, I called work and cancelled my trip.

I went from preparing to tour the world with a band, to full-on survival mode in just minutes.

I knew it was time to call in the troops, to bring Brianna's immediate family together, to bring in all the doctors, and to discuss what was going on. These were big ideas, and in the end, they would involve a full-family decision. With the severity, the urgency, there wasn't time to wait. It was time to act.

When you are with someone with a lifelong illness, hospital visits are more like doctor visits. Routine. You don't see hospitals like others do. But a lung transplant was out of the ordinary and important. At the same time, it was a difficult, complex topic. Her entire family had to be involved. And it was best if her family's questions could be asked directly and the information processed and compared right then. There was a lot of information, a lot of emotions, and a bit of panic. Having more brains around to help everyone comprehend meant a clearer understanding. An emergency family meeting with the doctors was crucial. Before I had hung up the phone with Dr. Pottinger, I had asked him to gather the doctors while I gathered Brianna's family. It was natural for me to be proactive, and this was one of those moments when being proactive was important.

A time was set. It was based on the doctors' schedules, not the family's, but getting all the doctors together was rare and nearly impossible. I called each family member, pleading for their attendance, telling them how this was a huge step. There was no accommodating people's schedules; this was it—one time and one time only. Through the confusion and complexity, Brianna's family got caught up on the news, the shock, and gathered to support her.

With Brianna's family and doctors gathered, it was time. It was a scary feeling for sure. Brianna was in her hospital bed, her sister sitting with her, usually easing the seriousness with laughter. Justin and Erica, Val and Jim, all gathered by the window away from the door. I sat on the other side of Brianna, holding her hand. I was probably squeezing it, not realizing I was doing it, as I prepared for the worst. The doctors lined up in chairs as they walked in: Dr. Dandekar, Brianna's lead CF doctor; Dr. Pottinger, her infectious disease doctor; Dr. Aitken, the president of the CF division of the UW clinic, followed by the on-call internal medicine specialist.

The room was filled with silence. Emotion. Frustration. Confusion. It was tense.

Brianna's family was anxious to hear the news, yet scared to face it. The doctors, knowing what was going to be said, were focused only on keeping Brianna healthy. How do you tell a family the options are running out, the moment is crucial, and what you recommend has little chance of success? Oh, and we need to address this now, before it's too late. Dr. Pottinger started by telling us the pseudomonas, the main CF bug, was raging active. It seemed to be the culprit causing the acute inflammation and infection. The drugs used to fight it weren't working. The improvement was not occurring like usual. The doctors still had hope, but their tools were running out. Therefore, they were looking at a transplant. Because of the abscessus, the only clinic available was the University of Pittsburg Medical Center Lung Transplant Center. It would be a one-year process post-transplant. We would probably have to move to Pittsburgh, wait for a lung, have the transplant, then wait for Brianna to be strong enough to travel back home.

But…with abscessus, the odds of Brianna making it out of the hospital were very slim.

It was the last resort, but possibly the only remaining option, since nothing was working and Brianna was deteriorating. If a transplant was something we would even consider, it was going to take some planning.

When the doctors finished, we drilled them with questions, all nearly impossible to answer:

- How much longer?

- How much time do we have?

- When would this happen?

- Can we even get there?

Doctors aren't fortune tellers. But they are scientists. They can only respond based on what they have seen, and even then, it is difficult because each person is different. There were so many variables. Really, it was just a matter of riding the wave, but it was also time to start making big decisions.

This meeting was crucial. The content was crucial, but it also helped us refocus on spending time with Brianna.

The doctors walked away, and the family was pretty quiet. But Brianna went right to work, running through the options, never giving an opinion. Trying to understand, everyone just wanted to do what Brianna wanted to do and offered their commitment to her no matter what she chose.

I went right to work figuring out how to make the transplant possible without moving to Pittsburgh. The rules dictated that you had to be within two hours of the clinic, so I researched medical flights that might accommodate that need when and if a lung became available.

After an additional week in the hospital, the doctors were comfortable sending Brianna home. I still needed to pay the bills, so I had accepted a two-week gig with the Dixie Chicks. I kept Facebook updated so my road family would be up to date with the difficult road ahead.

I left Brianna home with her family and ventured off to work, receiving a warm welcome from my road family. The child in me wanted to stay home, but the adult needed to pay the bills. Luckily, it was a quick trip, but long enough to earn enough money to see us through for a couple of months.

Chapter 16

THE JOURNEY HOME

With things becoming serious and the possibility of traveling to Pittsburgh for a transplant looming, I was always planning. My brother Chad introduced me to a friend who sells hay and was interested in expanding to our area. With Brianna's job, and her being well known in the horse community, we were well connected to the horse network in the Kitsap area. This opportunity would be huge, and a great way to earn income while we resided in Pittsburgh, if and when the transplant happened. I had a truck and picked up a large, flatbed trailer to haul hay. We had land to store it, and the connections in the community to know about it, so all we had to do was hire an employee to manage it while away.

I dragged Brianna with me to get the trailer. During the drive, I looked over at her. She was usually bubbly and talking about life, but she could barely keep her head up. Her color was changing; her attitude had darkened. It was like she knew something bad was coming.

Since I had the trailer, Chad had called, asking me to help him haul some logs. It was an overnight expedition, with several stops due to the logs' various locations. Almost without thought, I said I couldn't go—I had to be with Brianna. Up to that point, if I wasn't working, Brianna and I were inseparable. I never left her side. But when I refused Chad, Brianna spoke up and demanded I go. It took a minute to register. She said he needed help, and I needed to spend some time with my brother. I was shocked, but frankly, I needed the distraction, so I agreed. At the time, I didn't realize Brianna was rebuilding my bonds with other people, since I'd focused on her at the expense of my other relationships.

I called Brianna's dad and asked him to come take care of Brianna for the night. Then I headed to work with Chad as instructed by Brianna. How could I argue with her? I left hesitantly, but I did go. It was a great night. We spent about eight hours loading and hauling logs from several locations. We used walkie-talkies we had charged up to communicate and chat while hauling in separate vehicles.

As if Brianna's health issues weren't enough at this time, her best friend, support hero Bentley, had been having seizures; later, we would find out they were caused by an aggressively growing brain tumor. Brianna was the herd manager; I called myself the farm manager. I kept the farm operating while she did what she did best: manage our animals. Vet bills are expensive, but they are part of owning animals. I didn't challenge Brianna when she felt it was time to call the vet. After all, she was the practice manager of a veterinary clinic. Then, while I was off helping my brother, she called to tell me it was time to put Bentley down. This was a huge thing. Bentley was our best friend. Bentley was Brianna's hero. Putting him down would be hard.

Luckily, it wasn't an emergency, but with Bentley in pain, Brianna called to schedule a home visit so he could be put down at home. Bentley was loved by the whole family, and Jim and Val joined us when the vet came.

Before Maci showed up, we made a bed for Bentley. Brianna's parents and I were crying our eyes out. But when I looked over at Brianna, she had barely shed a tear. She just sat with that pale, stale look. Even Maci wept a bit as she explained every step of the procedure. First, an IV would be inserted that would relax Bentley. As he became motionless, yet still breathing, the next needle would be inserted, which would bring his heart to a complete rest. Lifeless. I didn't understand Brianna's reaction, or lack of reaction. Bentley was her best friend. They were inseparable.

Later that night, with Brianna back on the medications we were using to try to karate chop her illness, we faded into our pillow talk, both numb from putting Bentley down. She wasn't sure why she didn't cry, but she said she had a sense of happiness. He was no longer in pain, but her happiness was filled with confusion. We'd talked about burying Bentley and Brianna together, like Antony and Cleopatra, several times. Brianna made it clear if she passed before him that she wanted me to put him down so they could be buried together. Their love was very strong. Bentley always went everywhere with her, and if we ever left Bentley at home, Brianna thought about him constantly. She would often complain of missing him, and she was always excited to see him—and the rest of her animals—when she returned home. And boy were they all excited to see her. They usually knew when she was pulling up in the driveway. Her dad used to call him "Straightly" as a play on words from Bentley, to make fun of how he would bend in half, swinging his tail around, super-excited to see Brianna. On Sunday, April 30, 2017, we put Bentley down.

The next day it was time to leave for a gig. Mentally, a lot was happening at once. It was just a few days in Phoenix with the Zac Brown Band. Work was difficult to come by because most gigs were for several months, but the friends who usually hired me knew I needed to be home for Brianna; they helped with a flood of shorter gigs so I could continue to pay the bills, but also be home to care for Brianna.

The day after putting Bentley down, I went to Phoenix. It was not only a short gig, but also Phoenix was close enough to get home quickly if things with Brianna got worse.

I felt uncomfortable leaving for the gig. Brianna hadn't bounced back like she usually did. She wasn't her normal self and she had just lost Bentley. We lost Bentley. It was tough. Leaving her with her family made things a bit better, but I still felt odd.

It was just a week. I would be home in one week.

Arriving in Arizona, I went right to sleep, got up in the morning, and walked to the venue—just a normal day. I met the crew and checked out the assignment. It was a standard protocol side screen projection. Pretty easy for me—something that helped in a stressful time.

About halfway through the day, before I was all setup, Brianna's sister called. This was rare. Her sister and I talk on the phone, but not like this. Once again, things seemed out of place. They were taking Brianna to the hospital again. She said Brianna was, of course, full of laughter, cracking jokes, and her spirit was strong. Brianna played it off like it was completely normal, just another routine hospital visit. It was not. She had never gone back into the hospital so quickly before.

When I spoke with Brianna, she told me to stay put. I'd be home soon enough. But at this point, I needed to be home. My mind wasn't at work; it was with Brianna. Once again looking for a voice of reason, I reach out to Dr. Pottinger. I texted that it was urgent I speak to him. In a matter of minutes, he called. He had to walk out of a conference to call. "I feel like I need to be home right now. I'm in Arizona, and they are heading back to the hospital now." This time he told me things weren't good. Things weren't moving in the direction we wanted. I needed to get home as soon as possible to be with Brianna—she needed me.

I never thought twice. I went into the venue and grabbed my new crew chief Omar, whom I had just met that day, and laid it out. Things were bad at home. I had to go—now. I left them with a complete position to fill, and they had to pick up my slack.

I had never walked off a gig before. I was proud of always following through, finishing the gig no matter the struggle. I felt bad but hopped into an Uber and got on the phone with Alaska Airlines. The customer service rep answered, and I described my crisis, my urgent need to get home to Seattle on the next available flight. I was racing to get home to my wife who had a serious health situation.

The service rep got me on a flight, but I had very little time to get my stuff and get on the plane. Dashing right into my seat, I felt anxious, stressed, and emotional. During three hours of just sitting, I was trying not to panic, but I understood things were going in the wrong direction. I was preparing for the worst.

When I landed, my brother Chad met me at the airport to rush me to the hospital. I somehow beat Brianna and her family there. You see, a trip to the hospital was never really a rush. We all knew what it usually meant—an extended stay. So it involved more than loading up and going. There was a bit of packing—clothes, comfortable pajamas, clothes to wear home, games to keep yourself busy, her journals, books and magazines, and your own snacks. The ferry was first come, first serve, on an hour rotation, so it involved a wait most of the time.

On our drive from the airport to the hospital, Chad saw my worry, my stress, and my panic. He knew whatever was happening was serious. Brianna's family all knew since we had talked about her condition getting worse and her possibly needing a transplant. We knew the return to the hospital meant her medications were failing. Her bugs were resistant to the weapons in the arsenal the doctors were trying to fight them with. But Chad did not know all this, so I had to fill him in, which was difficult.

When I saw Brianna, my heart swelled. My brother even remarked on how my attitude made a complete 360 just by having her present, close. She had that effect on me. She brought a sense of relaxation, of comfort in a stressful situation. She was the only person I wanted to be with, be around. Just her presence was enough in my life.

This was the night of May 2, 2017. Having to wait until morning before the doctors could come in, we rested in the hospital room.

The next morning, Dr. Dandekar, Brianna's CF doctor, came into the room. Breathing heavily, he didn't seem very hopeful. The medications were not working. The plan was to try a new string of medications—heavy hitters—to see if they would help.

As the day was swallowed up by fight, confusion, and weakness, Brianna, her mom, and I relaxed in the room, just taking time for us and trying to distract ourselves from the situation.

Even with the new medications, things weren't getting better. They didn't seem to have turned things around. And Brianna continued to decline, so much so that they moved her into the ICU. At this point, her lungs were just hanging on. Her dad and family visited, helping to pass time. In true Brianna fashion, her condition wasn't bad enough to keep her back from being inspiring. Her brother-in-law's brother had been diagnosed with ALS, and part of that disease's progression is that the patient eventually needs a feeding tube. Hearing about this diagnosis, like nothing else was more important, Brianna grabbed her journal and wrote him a letter, sharing her newfound relationship with her feeding tube—she named it Peggy—and doing her magic in easing his mind about getting one installed.

The next morning, May 4, the doctors had more bad news. The new medications weren't working, and Brianna's lungs were in full failure. The doctors could continue the meds and try to fight, but knowing Brianna's quality over quantity philosophy, they felt her comfort was most important now, as we entered the last part of her journey. As Dr. Dandekar, her CF specialist, shared this news, he couldn't stop his emotions from building up and filling his eyes with sadness. This has to be the hardest part of a doctor's job—telling people there are no other options—that the end of the road is near.

It was once again time to bring Brianna's family together. Precious little time was left, so they should all have a chance to visit her, to be there for her one last time. While the family was being summoned, I called Brittany, her best friend, part of BBB (Brianna, Brittany, and Bonnie), to share the news that we were out of options, and that Brianna wanted her closest friends nearby.

Even though it was not yet confirmed, all signs indicated we were near the end. We were on the last call. All the ammunition the doctors had on the shelf, all the options available, had been stretched to the max, and with no positive results.

In these kinds of situations, it is difficult to allow reality in—you cling to hope. But at the same time, you understand the reality. We didn't want to sit there fighting for what wasn't going to get us anywhere.

As we waited patiently, family began to arrive. Brianna's mom was already there, and now her dad, brother, and sister came. We all just sat around Brianna, cracking jokes, sharing memories, all trying to distract her from the IV machine behind her pumping the last bit of hope through her bloodstream.

Brianna was using everything she had left to fight through. In such moments, I tend to become the caregiver, nurturer. It's just who I am. The planner. Looking ahead, reacting as needed. While I was trying to relax and take the opportunity to socialize, I was also brainstorming about what would need to be done next in my head. What would make things easier? What to do if...? What would be the most symbolic way home? What did Brianna want, need? Medically, what was required?

Dr. Dandekar and Dr. Aitken arrived. Dr. Pottinger called in via telephone since he was out of town. This was the dreaded moment. With heavy hearts, we discussed the reality of the matter. What was most important now wasn't the fight, but Brianna's comfort. As Dr. Dandekar took a breath, tears began to build, emotions choking his words, but he mustered up the courage to finally say it....

"As you know, we have been trying to fight these bugs for a while now, to no avail. We have run out of options; they aren't working." As a human, his emotions were building, his tears welling up, but as a doctor, he was trying to remain calm and share the news. "Her lungs are failing. It's time we focus on comfort."

As everyone absorbed the reality, we all felt overwhelming emotions. We thanked the team of doctors for everything they had done on this journey. In response, the doctors shared their admiration for Brianna, and how she had touched the entire team. As we all filled the room with hugs, and thanks, the reality sank in.

Brittany and Bonnie made their way to the hospital, bringing other close friends of Brianna's to spend some time with her.

After some time together, her family slowly went back home to process, adjust, and prepare for the next few days ahead.

Before Brittany and Bonnie showed up, Brianna's family had all left, leaving just Val, Brianna, and me. Both Val and I had our moments with Brianna. It was my "truth" time when I let my emotions out. It was really my true goodbye. Brianna held me close, as I knelt by her bedside, sobbing, trying to bust the words through. As I sobbed, she teared up, holding my face and softly joking about us going like Romeo and Juliet.

This was the moment my mom had been worried about way back when I had first told her Brianna had CF. She was concerned for her baby. But it had been an amazing life. I wouldn't have given up any of the pain if it meant giving up a moment with Brianna.

After Brittany, Bonnie, and a host of other friends showed up, we had to share Brianna. Everyone needed time with her.

I was thankful for Brianna's interactions with them, but at the same time, I selfishly desired more alone time with her. We all did. At least I had gotten what I needed out—I cried; Brianna shared her love for me and her thankfulness for everything I had done.

At this point, my job was assisting and providing opportunities for people to say their goodbyes, but at the same time, I had to play crowd control so Brianna wouldn't be suffocated, like my mom had been with the constant flow of well-wishers.

Susan, Bonnie's mom, was there taking care of Bonnie's kids. After a while, we invited Susan in since she was friends with Brianna's dad's family, the Oases. Brianna and Susan shared a deep spiritual connection with God.

Susan was at Brianna's bedside, grasping her hand, while I sat at Bri's feet, hand touching her leg, all to sync our hearts in feelings. You could feel Susan's calm, collected nature as she recited seemingly well-rehearsed words that nonetheless flowed with an overpowering, gut-wrenching emotion.

Susan looked into Brianna's eyes, and Brianna's sense of comfort rose, as did her bond with Susan. Brianna's eyes showed a sense of the hereafter, like she already had one foot inside heaven.

"I know I'm going home to Jesus," Brianna replied. "I'm peaceful, and I'm excited to take my first full breath of Jesus air." Living a life of never feeling a full breath—something we all take for granted—it was the simple things to look forward to. But like always, she ended with a joke, "But what will I do there?"

Susan responded with laughter, joking back that she hadn't been there yet, so she didn't know. But she told a story about a girl who had had a near-death experience; she saw the light but regained life, her time not being up yet. The story talked about the girl and her warm spirit, and how she had spent her brief time in heaven. She recounted how roses grew around Jesus as he talked with people in heaven who asked him to help the people they had left behind. When the girl came back, she said, "I will spend my time in heaven doing good on earth. And whenever you see a rose, you will know I'm talking to Jesus on your behalf."

Brianna lit up. "I'm going to do that too."

Susan responded, "Instead of a rose, your sign can be the trillium, your favorite flower." Brianna loved the trillium that grew in her parents' backyard.

Susan followed that by reading Colleen Hitchcock's poem "Ascension":

Ascension

And if I go,
while you're still here...
Know that I live on,
vibrating to a different measure,
—behind a thin veil you cannot see through.
You will not see me,
so you must have faith.
I wait for the time when we can soar together again,
—both aware of each other.
Until then, live your life to its fullest.
And when you need me,
Just whisper my name in your heart,
...I will be there.

When Susan finished reading the poem, she said, "Brianna, that's you."

As Susan offered this enlightenment, Bonnie and Brittany showed up. Susan was tasked with watching Bonnie's kids so Brittany and Bonnie could have time with Brianna. As they socialized, joked, laughed, and reminisced, Brianna still bright from her talk with Susan, glowed as she shared her love for Jesus and excitement for that first effortless breath of Jesus air. She shared amazing stories and asked the girls to take care of me, never complaining, never questioning her journey, just relying on her faith in Jesus.

As the sun went down, the room emptied, leaving just her mom and me.

When the sun came up on Friday, May 5, 2017, the world seemed beautiful. Calm. Peaceful. Outside, it was a sunny, bright day. We watched the UW rowing team train outside Brianna's window in Union Bay, a part of Lake Washington. We had agreed to wait for Friday morning before leaving the hospital, in a last-ditch effort to find a way to save Brianna. But when the doctors came around, it was clear that it was time to head home—time to get Brianna back to her childhood home so she could go peacefully in a place she loved, and where she wanted to take her last breath.

It was a somber moment, but I had to get to work helping organize Brianna's exit.

Brianna wanted her IVs removed before she went home. This was a small victory for Brianna. Sure, CF would take her life, but by no means would she allow it to run her life. Removing the IVs gave her a bit of freedom while her body shut down....

Brittany, Brianna's sister Kristen, her mom, and her dad were all present, socializing, laughing, and preparing for the big exit. Kristen helped Brianna get dressed and put makeup on. Brianna was going to leave that hospital on top of the world, dressed beautifully, with full makeup, and full of dignity. Once again she owned the situation and was in full control. So much so, when we confirmed if she wanted to make a last stop at the Strand Family Farm, in Brianna fashion, she responded with "Can we stop and get tacos?" We all laughed. A way to, I guess, lighten the reality of the meaning of the question, as we joked about the idea of taking an ambulance through the drive-thru.

The plan was to take an ambulance to facilitate the oxygen and to stop at our home, the Strand Family Farm, in Port Orchard so Brianna could say her last goodbyes to the animals. Brittany had gone ahead to pull Dolce out and help use up some of her energy before Brianna arrived.

Brianna's niece Rylee Jo was with us, so she hopped into the ambulance to be with Brianna as well. This allowed Rylee and Brianna to have such a beautiful talk. Rylee was anxious and excited to ride in an ambulance, yet she was processing the emotions from a kid's perspective, trying to absorb the reality of what was happening. Brianna was always great with her niece and absolutely adored Rylee. From the time Rylee was born, Brianna had always been there for her, having sleepovers and spending girl time with just the two of them.

As we rode, I held Brianna's hand, admiring the way she talked with Rylee. It was as if she had it planned. With her strength and her leadership-inspiring ways, she gave Rylee four things to remember:

- Keep a smile on your face.
- Always eat dessert first.
- Never let Jim (Brianna's dad) teach you how to drive.
- And you are like a sister to me, not my little niece; I love you.

We pulled up to our little piece of paradise. The weather was beautiful—the sun was shining, and there was enough wind to keep the trees dancing. As we pulled up, the animals came out. Thankfully, they had been cared for by Brianna's amazing clinic staff volunteering their time to help support in this time of need.

In the lead was Dolce. As Brianna got out of the ambulance, Brittany led Dolce over. Dolce was inspecting, smelling, understanding, as Brianna loved on Dolce and said her goodbyes. It was tough, emotional. Here we had built this home together, a paradise, our palace, and it was sinking in that this was the last time Brianna would be here. Brianna was the heart of this place.

After putting Dolce back in her stall, Brianna loved on the kitties. Then we loaded her back into the ambulance and ventured along to Brianna's parents' home...and the end of Brianna's journey.

We tucked Brianna into bed, getting her comfortable, away from her CF, away from the abscessus, away from the hospital, and most importantly, close to her entire family. Everyone knew it was the end, so they all came to camp out at her bedside, taking advantage of every breath left in her. Her sister's entire family, her brother's family, her mom and dad—everyone was there. It was beautiful. We all took turns spending time with her. Socializing, laughing, caring for her, and just being with her.

At the same time, Brianna was saying her last words to us. She had an individual message for each person. It was very magical—as if she had rehearsed them all. Her most frequent sentiment was that everyone needed be one with God and have faith in Jesus. As a challenge, Brianna said she would be waiting for them in heaven.

And, as throughout our entire relationship, she told everyone this was not goodbye, but see you soon.

Eventually, we all fell asleep. We were all extremely drained. The hospital stay had been about a week, and no one had been able to sleep well.

For me, this experience was extreme. I had never seen a person die. I had watched my mom get close, but I had said goodbye the night before she passed. Never had I experienced the last breath. I was trying to stay aware of everything, but at the same time, I was nervous, scared, and everything but emotional. I guess, in my mind, I had already let my emotions flow and said my goodbyes. Plus, the numerous nights of pillow talk and difficult discussions throughout our relationship had helped build me up for this moment. I was in caring, nurturing mode.

On Saturday, May 6, 2017, Brianna's weakness was showing. Her body was shutting down. About mid-day, the sun broke through the clouds. I asked Brianna what she wanted for her last meal—she wanted pizza—her favorite food—and root beer. Pizza was definitely her favorite, along with tacos.

Brianna didn't want to go outside when we first asked her. She was tired. Going outside would mean she'd need assistance, and once again, that took away some of her independence. She didn't like that. After sometime, somehow, she was ready to go outside. I lifted her up out of bed and carried her through the front door—almost as if I was carrying her through the threshold to the start of her new journey home to heaven. We sat her into a wheelchair, parked her in the middle of the grass, and within moments, the sun shone brightly on her, like a spotlight. It was one of those peaceful, belief-inspiring times. Time slowed down for once. It was beautiful.

Rylee had a gymnastic event coming up, so she got to show Brianna her routine. With a full smile, Brianna watched with a slice of pizza in her hand. It was magical. We all just sat around Brianna as the sun shined on her and gave a light of peace.

A lot of people wanted to see Brianna. Her dad was updating everyone on Facebook as they checked in on Brianna.

As the sun went down, her friends left, and it was just the immediate family again. We were all on edge when Brianna summoned her energy and called everyone into her room. She was barely able to hold her eyes open or hold her head up. She could barely speak clearly—not from being tired, but because her brain was shutting down as her lungs gave way....

"Tomorrow," she began, "I probably won't wake up, so I want to tell you guys how much I love you, how much you guys mean to me."

It was like she knew it was that time. She was in control once again and confident. The family was in tears, trying to process the emotions. She was sitting, legs crossed, trying to fight falling asleep. Her head would be up, eyes closed; then she'd have a moment when her body would give and she'd catch herself mid-fall, much like when someone is falling asleep sitting up and trying to fight it. It was extremely tough to watch this. I was on one side, and Justin was on the other. We all knew once she fell asleep, her mind wouldn't be waking up again. And at the same time, we were admiring how she was fighting so hard...so hard. Finally, after some time watching and asking her multiple times in different ways, to no avail, if she wanted to lie down, I gently eased her back, resting her head on the pillow.

Once lying down, her last words, with the voice of the fight within them, were, "All you had to do was ask."

I couldn't help but chuckle, but at the same time, I realized what had just happened. She was fighting. Sitting up was her holding on, like the little fighter she was.

As she lay back, we all just watched as she gasped for every last breath.

We spent the night taking turns watching over her. Her brother read her a book and talked to her. It was nearly impossible to sleep. With every little sound, we would all jump up to see if it was her last words or last breath. The emotions were heavy; we were all extremely tired, emotionally drained, and worn out.

Once she laid down, finally, her body never moved much again. At this point, it was just her vital organs resting, snuggling into the last breath. Justin and I lay by her side that night. The rest of the family was not far away, spread around the many rooms of the house. We were all extremely exhausted from this journey, from the last week's battle, to even computing the last twenty-nine years with her. We were all tired, doing all we could to get sleep, yet struggling not to close our eyes, afraid of missing something, maybe another push of consciousness, words, or even just her last breath.

Her breathing became shallower and shallower. Justin and I rotated, administering her meds, dancing the fine line between keeping her comfortable and allowing the process to happen naturally.

She was unable to talk, but she still registered our words, taking an extra deep gasp of air every time we spoke to her.

Being a fighter, Brianna held on through Sunday. She spent the entire day lying motionless. Restless, her dad left in the morning, to play his regular position of lead guitar at the Sunday service. As night fell, Sunday was wrapping up, and the week was about to begin. Kristen told Brianna her family had to go, but she would be back in the morning. Talking to Brianna, knowing she was listening to every word, Kristen finished reassuring Brianna and asked her dad to lead a prayer.

Jim usually led the family prayers, always finding the perfect words. In this prayer, he released Brianna to Jesus. He said we couldn't do any more, and there was no one better to lift her up to.

As the prayer came to a close, Brianna opened her eyes and she took two deep breaths....

On Sunday, May 7, 2017, around 9:00 p.m., Brianna finished her journey on earth—and graduated to heaven.

Her body was motionless, but her soul was lifted up to Jesus. Her passing was beyond beautiful. Somehow, her power made it slow. Always selfishly wanting more time, we were blessed with perfect closure. Honestly, it couldn't have been any more beautiful. Brianna, now officially an angel, returned to Bentley and all the others who had passed before her, finishing the mission she was sent to accomplish and leaving a legacy that will be remembered forever.

Chapter 17

GOD'S GREAT DANCE FLOOR

After Brianna's passing, things were difficult, as one might imagine. We had never thought this day would come so soon. We knew it would be here eventually, but this soon caught us all off guard a bit. I was trying to do what I could to recalibrate my reality, my busy mind processing all that transpired, trying to adjust to a new, forced, uncomfortable, and confusing normal.

As with anything else, I went right to work. Had to. Right after Brianna passed, Chad came to get me.

It was nice to get away and spend some time at my brother's place. Grieving wasn't the first thing I thought about. I was excited in a way to plan Brianna's celebration. There would be no funeral—that wasn't Brianna's style. No, it would be a celebration. My love for Brianna radiated through me, and there was no greater honor than to match that energy in her celebration—to celebrate the legacy she created and share my love for her.

We knew the venue for the celebration would be her family's church, which she grew up attending. Her faith was strong and the root of her power.

Looking at the calendar, one date jumped off the page. There could be no better time to celebrate Brianna than the day of the CF walk: June 3, 2017.

The timing was almost perfect, just a month after Brianna's passing. Here, in her superhuman way, with her devotion to the CF Foundation, and to her legacy, Brianna was pulling people together not only to celebrate her, but also to continue advocating for CF awareness and raising money in the mission to make CF stand for Cure Found. The event was such a success; the numbers overshot the $28,000 raised in 2016. In full BriLiever fashion, we raised more than $45,000.

I knew I owed it to Brianna to make the event amazing, plus my love for her demanded nothing less. We live our lives, many years long, creating our legacy, interacting with everyone around us. We all only pass once, and we come together as a whole only once to celebrate the person's life. This was our only chance. Forever we remember, but only once do we celebrate it as a whole congregation.

No way would I let Brianna down for her celebration. She was my best friend, the love of my life, my soul partner. I had spent eleven years with her, teaming up to conquer a disease—conquer life— and I had one chance to show off her life's legacy. Plus, it was a way for me to control my energy; it was what I love to do. And I got to brag about the one I so adored.

We recorded the entire event, and streamed it live to those who couldn't make it. The venue was packed, holding just over 800 people—an equal number of people logged on to watch. When it was time to start, nervous as could be, I walked through the lobby, seeing faces we hadn't seen in a long time—some faces were a complete surprise. Many who walked up to me said, "I don't know you, and never got to know Bri, but just by knowing of her, we were inspired by her and her strength."

Brianna's pictures, memories—displays of her amazing life—lined the walls, completely filling the lobby. There wasn't enough room to display all the memories she had somehow crammed into her twenty-nine years.

Brittany, Bonnie, and Katie, a close childhood friend, did an amazing job of bringing out her character in pictures and showcasing every achievement.

As you walked into the auditorium, just in front of the stage, the space was filled with all things Brianna. Brianna's mom had gathered a group of friends to pay this tribute to her. A mannequin wore Brianna's wedding dress, beautifully stretched out onto the stairs to fully display its princess glow. Her FFA jackets were displayed on other mannequins, reflecting her leadership in National Blue and Corn Gold. An easel showcased her two big diplomas in crimson and gray, the WSU logos, and of course, there was a picture of Brianna and her beautiful smile, showing excitement about her achievements. Her saddle from all the years riding and sharing her love for animals was on display, along with her high school graduation cap and gown, her neon-green WSU sweatshirt that screamed her character, and a number of pictures exemplifying her many layers of beauty.

To the side was a five-foot canvas of Brianna's powerful picture. It was a print of the original of her at the house, in the field, the same one used for this book's cover, with her glow radiating, as a light shone on her.

On stage was my biggest work. For two weeks prior to the celebration, I had collected numerous sheets of cardboard, spending many hours crafting and perfecting to create amazing four-foot, three-dimensional letters that were placed all the way across the stage. The edges were done in Seahawks blue, and of course, the main color was neon green. Completely catching your attention as you walked in, they spelled out: B-R-I-A-N-N-A, spanning across the entire stage.

The stage was set for a beautiful presentation. And that's just what it was.

We enlisted Jim's band, Sweet T & Justice, including some of the church's musicians, to perform numbers to help break up the speakers a bit. The performance that stood out the most was played in the middle of the celebration: an amazing, beautiful rendition of the Dani and Lizzy song "Dancing in the Sky." The lead singer of Brianna's dad's band, Theresa, belted out the notes, making us feel like we were all in heaven with Brianna as she asked about heaven's amazing qualities, while lamenting that the good stuff went with her and left an emptiness behind here on earth.

Our speakers were people from Brianna's life who had helped shape her amazing story. Each and every one of them shared memories of Brianna, all describing her the same way without even communicating with one another before the event: comfort, joy, energy, glow, hero, beauty. They all felt her legacy would live on, as she shared the same energy with everyone she was bless to interact with.

Pastor Tom, a close family friend, officiated. He led everyone in prayer, compared the definition of a hero to Brianna, and invited the speakers on stage.

Dr. Bonnie Ramsey from the children's hospital, Brianna's first CF doctor, said every time Brianna came into the clinic, she had a plan, she had spirit, and she blossomed and thrived when CF treatment finally started. She never let CF stop her. Having a full family of support, she was beautiful, radiating joy, energy, and spirit—it was like she glowed. Dr. Ramsey concluded, "Brianna made all of our lives just a little bit better, just by knowing her."

John Waller, Brianna's high school teacher and FFA chapter advisor, said when she would talk, everyone listened. So much so that she was elected as the Washington State FFA secretary, all for a speech about her favorite shoes: Georgia Boot Romeos.

He said she was a glass always half full; first to arrive, last to leave; first with an encouraging word; a born leader; the best to bring-out the best; and a lead-by-example kind of girl.

And he simply said thank you:

Thank you for letting us into your life.

Thank you for being a positive person, even in the face of adversity.

Thank you for sharing that incredible smile and your never-ending faith.

Thank you for being a beautiful, incredible role model for both young and old.

Thank you for being a voice of encouragement in everything that is life.

Thank you for making each and every one of us a little bit better by just knowing you.

Dottie Vlasuk, director of the Washington chapter of the Cystic Fibrosis Foundation, said Brianna was an outstanding spokesperson for the foundation, always free in telling her personal story no matter how intimate it was. She said Brianna wanted others to really get a sense of what it was like to live with cystic fibrosis, and she also wanted to get them to participate in helping fund CF research.

Dr. Paul Pottinger, the infectious disease doctor and one of Brianna's biggest advocates, said her body was just not a match for her spirit and soul. All his patients had their own stories, but Brianna's was different. She was spectacular, extraordinary, inspiring, and unique. No one else came close to her. She simply wanted people to understand her experience so others could have a better shot in the future. That was classic Bri, right? It was not about her. It was about volunteering to do something for someone else.

"I've just never met anybody like that," said Dr. Pottinger. "And I've been a doctor since 1998, so I've met a lot of folks. In the end, Brianna's body was not nearly a match for her spirit and her soul and her true inner self."

Maci and Jasmin, the two vets Brianna worked for at Clover Valley Veterinary, gave her an honorary veterinarian degree, for her devotion to animals through her leadership through the clinic.

A letter from US State Senator Patty Murray, and words from Poulsbo Mayor Becky Erickson were read.

Susan Ogilvie, a family friend, said we were all here to celebrate Brianna, but we were really celebrating the foundation of what Brianna was and her amazing legacy of family, faith, love, friendship, and hope.

Brianna's three close friends—Katie, Brittany, Bonnie—stressed the task Brianna had set for them of finding Jesus so she could be with them in heaven, and to simply take care of me and help me through the tough times ahead. Knowing Brianna's love for coffee, they promised, every year, in the first week in May, to have S'mores Frappuccino, Brianna's favorite, during Starbucks' frappe hour.

Brianna's sister-in-law Erica said it was an honor to be part of Brianna's journey. "Just to know her, was to love her."

Her brother Justin shared their similarities—their many random vivid dreams, random sounds from their throats, and their amazing journeys to Nicaragua, and their drive up from Texas. He laughed about Brianna insisting on using a real map instead of the GPS, and using her silly books to find weird roadside attractions and strange places to eat. He talked about when his family had lived with Brianna and me, and smelling Brianna cooking tacos. Bri wanted us all to be comfortable.

Her sister Kristen shared stories of her daily talks with Brianna and a letter she wrote to Brianna.

Her niece Rylee shared how much she was the spitting image of her Auntie Bri, full of sass, energy, and spark. She said Brianna always made her feel special, loved spending time with her, and was always encouraging and positive. She loved all her memories and loved all the animals Brianna had. "Whenever she said I love you, she meant it a lot," Rylee said.

Her mom shared Brianna's power quotes, specifically ones from Brianna's Facebook "About" section, created back in 2010, still present on her Facebook page today:

> I'm wacky and chill, a little crazy and goofy, opinionated and stubborn, and moody at times, but I always like to have a good ol' time and live life to the absolute limit! I was born and raised a country girl who tries her best to abide in the Father and will forever be that way! I love being with my family and miss them so much—my friends are incredible, new and old! I love animals, especially my horses, cows and dog (a good hint to why that's my major); I love the simple things in life, love to have fun and to go dance the night away! I also like stayin' in and watchin' movies. I love food...any food and crave espresso 24/7! I love readin' and have an uncanny thirst for knowledge. I love being with my other half, and I am so incredibly psyched to become an aunt for the first time this December!

Jim, Brianna's dad, praised Brianna's faith and her strength in the days leading up to her death.

After everyone else spoke, I shared my love for Brianna. With a script, nervous in front of crowds, I shared my amazing memories, realizations, and absolute affection. I wanted to give Brianna the best world ever, just to be blessed with her smile. That was my gift in life—to see her smile every day.

When I finished speaking, the celebration concluded with Brianna's favorite song.

How that song was chosen takes a little bit of explanation. Most can't even talk about dying. It's not an easy topic, but Brianna and I had talked about it many times. So much so that she almost had the entire celebration planned out early in our relationship. She always talked about how *if* she passed, she wanted it to be a party. She wanted to dance! She wanted laughter, no tears or sadness.

We would sit together in bed, her notebook out with a list of fun questions, her and her unique personality always replacing discomfort with laughter. We'd roll through the questions, both answering as she logged them in her journals. She asked questions like "What's your favorite color? What are your favorite foods? Of each other's families, who are you most comfortable with? What songs do we wanted played at our funerals?" Most of the time, these questions stumped me since they involved thought and character. But every time I asked her, she knew the answers. Her favorite song for her celebration—because she wanted everyone to dance with her and celebrate—was "God's Great Dance Floor" by Chris Tomlin.

A few years back, Brianna's dad had shared with us some tickets to Chris Tomlin at the Key Arena in Seattle. From the concert to the many times in the car, every time she played the song it was so upbeat, in the spirit Brianna admired about Jesus.

As a master planner who always goes over the top, I knew that song would be played at the end, and I would get everyone to dance to it. But I wasn't going to settle for a recording. Being in the music industry, I have connections. I tracked down Chris Tomlin's manager and sent him an email asking if he would be interested in performing that song for Brianna. Unfortunately, it conflicted with his schedule. But that didn't mean we couldn't have a live performance of that song.

As the evening concluded, the band started to play "God's Great Dance Floor." Rolling through the first chorus, the family joined the band as we all sang along. The song is upbeat, with a fast tempo that makes it hard not to dance. We gathered on stage and called everyone to join us.

Nervous, excited, and holding back my joy, I announced, "It has been a blessing to have so many people touch our lives. And to hear from those who have been touched and continue to be touched by Brianna, her amazing journey, and her love for life and God. We all knew she was and is something special. But never did we ever imagine she was this inspiring, leaving such a legacy. So, in her honor, as requested by her, to finish this celebration of life, please, let's make it a party. And let's all stand up. Sing loud, dance hard, give it all you got. And let the world know how much we all loved and continue to love her."

The entire room stood, danced, and sang.

We completely fulfilled her wish—there was no better feeling.

I always loved making Brianna smile and going over the top for her. It was in my blood, the only way I knew how to do things, and just a joy. And for sure, I knew her heart was on fire, her smile was bright like always, and best of all, she was taking every full breath of air with ease, no pain. So much so that the morning of her celebration, I woke in uplifting tears. The dream was extremely clear and visual. I rarely remember my dreams, but this one I can remember clearly to this day. Brianna and I were walking through a field. The sun was shining so brightly, blocking my view of her.

The field was full of wildflowers—Brianna's favorite: trilliums.

Brianna was letting me know she was with me.

Brianna was a superhero to many. She seemed so strong and powerful while battling such a debilitating disease. What most people don't know is her struggles started before she was born. During her pregnancy, Brianna's mom Val suffered extreme pain, landing her in the hospital. Doctors diagnosed Val with a burst ovarian cyst. They recommended an abortion because of what the burst could do to an unborn child, but her family declined and prayed for healing. God provided Brianna, free of any defects caused by the burst cyst. However, the family genes they were unaware of had instead passed on CF.

Brianna was born on May 11, 1988, weighing seven pounds, eleven ounces.

Her name means the strong one, strong, virtuous, and honorable.

Here's what's crazy about this story. Yes, Brianna was powerful. But sometimes we don't learn how powerful a person is until they leave us. After Brianna passed and the celebration came near, we were looking through pictures and memorabilia for the celebration and came across some very amazing things. Brianna loved to document her days on a calendar and write in her journals. As we went through these pictures and writings, we started to connect some extremely powerful dots.

Keep in mind, Brianna's favorite numbers were seven and eleven. I did not realize until then the extreme power behind the two numbers. Our proposal date was 1-7-11; we got married on 7-11-11. Her favorite numbers became a thing.

Our anniversary was a big thing for us, so much so that 7 Eleven loved to celebrate it, too, with free Slurpees for 7/11 day. It made for a fun adventure for our anniversary every year.

Brianna's birthday was May 11. On May 7, 2017, Brianna took her last breath and graduated to heaven. Her favorite numbers played out on each end of her life. She was born on the eleventh and passed on the seventh, just four days prior to her twenty-ninth birthday—close enough to say she was twenty-nine, so we always have. I guess if you count the nine months in her mom's womb, she just missed her thirtieth birthday. A goal she had often voiced was to live to her thirtieth birthday.

On Brianna's side of the bed, in her bedstand, Brittany found her journals. Brianna loved to write. She loved her journals. While we were married, I never really read what she wrote since it was her thing. But what we found was beautiful.

In one of the smaller flip notebooks, we found something she had written on every page—something she was thankful for about me.

You push me to be a better person!

You are very
supportive of my
career!

You don't put up
w/ my sh@t!

Family is every-
thing to you!

your loud and goofy nature.

You don't get scared
when I talk about
death.

I love that you love to visit me at work!

You don't even notice
or care what other
people think!

You appreciate my need for animals. And perpetuate that need :)

Your kindred
spirit!

You know me better than anyone in the world.

You love my best friend and even call her when I'm not around.

You love to
surprize me...
ie our honeymoon

You understand my
love of coffee...
and are ok with it!

The way your eyes
smile before your
lips even do

Your 10 year
plan for us — when
we hadn't even
started dating!

The softness of
your lips!

All you want to
do is make me happy
and your actions
always show me that!

I'm jealous that you are more romantic and thoughtful than me."

You are always
trying to solve problems
and make things
better

You're ok with
my love of food

You understand that life is an adventure!

You are a steak
and potatoes guy!

You make my
heart pitter patter!

You are the first thing I thank God for every night when I close my eyes and say my prayers.

You don't drink
alcohol.

You are real with
me when we talk
about my CF.

Continuingly flipping through these pages, I was amazed, emotional. To this day, I still read them in awe. As I continued through, I turned back to the one about our ten-year plan. "Your ten-year plan for us when we hadn't even started dating."

In 2007, as the convention grew closer, we had talked more and more. After expressing my feelings, I had shared with her my ten-year plan. I was a bit of a planner even then. But maybe I should have made a twenty-, thirty-, or forty-year plan, maybe longer. In 2007, I told her about my ten-year plan. She passed in 2017. We had spent exactly ten years together. We originally met in 2006, so we knew each other for eleven years. But we were inseparable for ten.

Now it goes even deeper. In one of the journals we found a devotional. "Commit to the Lord whatever you do, and your plans will succeed. PROVERBS 16:3." In the many lines below, she wrote in her answer:

> I love to be around people and to give speeches, even though I get nervous, to be a spokesperson for CF and get to spread awareness to everybody would be very neat, and it would help a lot of people. Being a doctor would be about the same because I could really relate to the kids and what they are going through. I like to make people happy. I plan to be married by twenty-three, and want to have kids by age twenty-five. I know that sometimes things don't go as planned, but I am not going to let my disease stop me.

Commit to the LORD whatever you do, and your plans will succeed.

Proverbs 16:3

I love to be around people & to give speeches even though I get nervous. To be a spokesperson for CF and get to spread awareness to everybody would be very neat and it would help a lot of people. Being a doctor would be about the same because I could really relate to the kids and what they are going through. I like to make people happy. I plan to be married by 23 & want to have my first kid by age 25. I know that sometimes things don't go as planned, but I am not going to let my disease stop me.

Here's what's crazy. Brianna definitely pinpoints her strengths, but also plans to be married at age twenty-three. She was, in fact, twenty-three when we got married.

Nope, not done. Having kids was a constant topic. We both loved kids. I think maybe we loved animals more, but we both definitely wanted kids. Cystic fibrosis made this dream extremely difficult. With the disease causing heavy mucus, it made it very difficult for sperm to get to the uterus. That's if the meds didn't kill them, or even if the meds hadn't messed with the uterus. Added to that were reproductive difficulties that would keep a perfectly healthy human from conceiving. Now let's say Brianna was able to get pregnant; she'd have to know almost immediately to have any chance of stopping the meds before they kicked the fertilized egg out. Then, let's say she got past this stage, and a baby formed. The odds of the mother living through the birth were low. When we saw a high-risk fertility doctor, we were told the mother should be at about a 60 percent lung function or more. At the time of our appointment, Brianna was already down to 55 percent. So, all these issues considered, it was very unlikely we could ever make it to the finish line, let alone pass it. We talked about a surrogate, whom it might be, and who would be willing to physically, mentally, and even financially do it for us. Having a child seemed like a pipe dream.

Then, on a July morning in 2013, when Brianna was twenty-five, I heard her crying in the bathroom. It caught me off-guard. When I entered the bathroom, instead of words, she showed me a pregnancy test. It had a plus sign. She was pregnant. What a joy it was to feel that. To be a dad. To create a human with someone you love. There's no greater gift.

Most wait to tell family. But this was a first for Brianna. Brianna wanted to tell her family right away. I wanted to tell her family! It kept her smile beaming. We raced over to her parents' house that night. Of course, we didn't just spill the beans. I had taken a picture of Brianna holding the test. I placed it in a photo album on my phone. I can't remember what it was an album of, but I had randomly placed the picture in it. I showed the album to her mom and dad. They were both sitting on the couch. Her dad was holding the phone, swiping through each photo as her mom looked over his shoulder. Next, next, next…. Of course, her dad missed the picture. After a couple of photos passed by, her mom caught on. "Wait, go back." He swiped back to the picture. Her mom knew what it was and screamed for joy, while jumping up and down. Then her dad finally caught on!

The excitement didn't last long. Three days later, Brianna's body expelled the baby. It was hard. But it had been a blessing to experience the excitement and joy of being pregnant. If you remember, Brianna's devotional stated she would have kids at age twenty-five. Brianna was twenty-five when she got pregnant.

And there's more. Bentley was put down on April 30. Brianna passed on May 7, exactly seven days later. Clearly, Brianna was emotionless when putting Bentley down because she knew Bentley had crossed the Rainbow Bridge just ahead of her and was waiting for her. At the end of her red carpet, the procession had guided the two back together only a week later up in heaven. And as requested, we buried the two together, as Brianna always dreamed of.

LET'S RECAP:

- Favorite numbers: 7 & 11.

- Born: May 11, 1988.

- Passed: May 7, 2017.

- Ten-year plan: 2007-2017 = 10 Years

- Met in August of 2006 starting convention planning Fall 06: 11 years (2006-2017).

- Devotional calls for marriage at age 23 (2011), pregnant at age 25 (2013).

- Married at age 23 (7-11-2011).

- Pregnant (but miscarried) at age 25 (2013).

- Bentley, her best friend, put down April 30, 2017: 7 days before Brianna passed.

- Now I don't know if you noticed how many chapters there were in this book, but just because seven and eleven were her favorite numbers, the book took eighteen chapters to complete her story. Seven plus eleven equals eighteen.

- To finish, Brianna, being full of faith, hope, and love for Jesus, passed on May 7, 2017, a Sunday, the seventh day, just like when God rested.

Brianna never pushed her religious belief onto people. She led by example. One of those examples was her power of prayer. Now, as if all the sevens and elevens weren't enough, looking back at the religious connection of seven and eleven in the Bible, we find Matthew 7:7-11, "Ask and you will receive. Search and you will find. Knock and the door will be opened for you. Everyone who asks will receive. The one who searches will find, and for the one who knocks, the door will open." The power of prayer.

Brianna's life was all about beating the odds. First, her mother had been advised against giving birth to Brianna; then Brianna was diagnosed with cystic fibrosis. But this diagnosis helped her family focus on the power of prayer, which helped them become tighter, closer, and to live every day to the fullest, full of laughter, love, and devotion. This created a Brianna with no fear, lots of confidence, and superhuman strength, who could stand up to the scariest thing: Death. It made her passing such a beautiful journey. Although we were sad to have her leave us, Brianna was fearless in joy for her journey to heaven.

All her life, Brianna continued the effort to leave a legacy. And that she did. Going back and listening to her retirement address from FFA, playing it back over her slideshow from the end of her celebration, I realized how completely she had covered her entire life almost ten years before it was finished. Her connection was so strong that she knew the entire time why she was here on earth and where she was going.

Note:

Video of Brianna's celebration is available at
ChooseYourAttitude.org/BriMazing.

Chapter 18

CHOOSE YOUR ATTITUDE, CREATE YOUR LIFE

Once the celebration was over, as things slowed way down, it all hit me. Thankfully, my road family stayed intact. Many of them reached out to offer love and support. Around this time, the Tim Mc-Graw and Faith Hill Soul 2 Soul tour came to the Tacoma Dome. Because they had a large road family pool on that run and had heard what had happened, they invited me out to see everyone and to remind me that my road family was still solid, despite all the new confusion I had at home.

Luckily, Brianna and I, before her passing, had been working on designing a new deck for the house; the old one had been falling apart since we bought the place. As a way to stay busy and occupied, directly after the celebration, I spent two-and-a-half weeks, sun up to sun down, working on the deck, with some rare appearances from friends and family to help, but for the most part, alone, by myself, putting my heart and soul into building the most beautiful deck ever, just like I did with everything else for Brianna.

The deck was a beautiful distraction. Brianna's smile was my fuel for life. In a way, I was still burning on that desire. When it was all said and done, although the deck was beautiful, gorgeous, and extremely peaceful, my true reason for building it wasn't around. It was lonely. Quiet. Unsatisfying. I wasn't finding my desire. My close family and friends said I needed to sell the place. At first, I was instantly offended. It was extremely hard to hear. I guess I was still riding the fuel—her presence that I felt from the celebration, from distraction.

When the dust settled from the construction, I realized they were right. With nothing for me to do, the farm got extremely silent. Bentley wasn't around to follow me everywhere; Brianna wasn't there to love on, talk to, or be smothered by in her comfort. There was only the wind, the noises of nature. It was too much to take care of. The farm no longer served its purpose. I had no desire to remain. Even with the most beautiful deck ever built, it wasn't enough to make me stay.

I sold the place and moved away. It felt good to hear the inspector's admiration when he heard the deck was built privately, not professionally; he even said it exceeded some professional builds.

I moved away in search of a new life, new friends, a new place to call home—in search of me. Brianna had been my everything. I didn't have many friends; she was my everything. Her friends were my friends. But socializing without Brianna by my side was extremely hard—I was way out of my element.

After the celebration of life, after your loved one has been sent on their way, for some reason, death makes families, friends scatter. Clam up. Hide from feelings, emotions. Everyone wanted to be strong, yet they were weak or fragile and had a hard time feeling that way around others. Friends and everyone you run into, as soon as you see them, ask how you're doing, yet they struggle to find words. It's tough.

We all handle things differently. I understood that; however, still being human, to this day, I struggle to mediate between my understanding and my direct emotions. There was a lot of processing. The adult me understood others' awkwardness, yet the child in me was hurt by unintended actions due to their own discomfort.

Life was difficult. Brianna had been my comfort zone. There was no life issue too small for her to tackle. And really, she didn't have to do much work. Her voice, her presence, and her superhuman glow gave me comfort and always made me feel safe. But that was all gone now. My mom was gone. They were my safe zones. Nurturers. Gone. I was alone.

There were lots of changes, and I just did all I could to keep moving, trying to put my life back together. I continued working. Distractions. Thankfully, work kept me busy. But still, it was difficult.

Our journey had been a beautiful one. Much like the song "Big Yellow Taxi" by Joni Mitchell, you don't realize what you have until it's gone. We all knew Brianna was beautiful, but we didn't really understand the scale, and it continues to flourish. Sometimes, I still discover revelations, signs of her beautiful spirit. And sometimes, it's intense feelings of absence. Her strength inspired many aspects of my life—who I am. The lessons I learned were simple, yet constants every time we interacted.

As I tried to process everything, I gathered my thoughts, my understanding of all we had been through, and tried to remember her biggest message. Everything was about helping people through their journey. No matter how you feel about the afterlife, you're still losing someone on earth. Their presence. But for me, it's about remembering and reminding myself I'm the sad one. She's gone, but she is feeling free of the struggle she did so well at concealing from the world.

If you have CF, know that being diagnosed and/or born with CF, you're not simply a statistic. You are something more. Each one of you has your unique story. It's okay to take ownership of your independence. At the same time, try not to get lost in the hourglass; don't hide the expiration date. Embrace it. Use it as inspiration for meeting your goals. Be honest about your health. Somehow, Brianna was able to embrace it and move forward. The health system is slow. In our minds, things feel like they need an acute response. Some things do; however, healing takes time. I remember many times doctors reminding us to look at weeks and months—days are too soon.

Doctors, know that your work is never unrecognized; your job is important, and we value that. You are taught how to fix things or respond to things in a scientific environment, but please keep in mind that you're fixing a human being. Human beings have minds, hearts, souls, and lives. In your eyes, you're trying to fix a health issue. In their minds, they are just trying to live. Please never lose focus of that as you try to find middle ground between science and humanity. Humans need to live and build strength, and to find hope and motivation, and sometimes that comes by pushing back, stopping a disease from overpowering them. Sometimes they just want to bust free.

Prescribe some freedom with your solution. Science may say ten hours of procedures, twenty-four-hour IVs. But patients aren't experiments. Make sure to truly listen. What doesn't make sense to you scientifically may make complete sense to them.

Friends and family, know that disease is difficult for all involved. Spend time with people now. Early. Be a part of their fight. Talk to them. Not everyone is willing to be vulnerable like Brianna was, so be patient. And a lot of the times, people are overwhelmed with the information around what's happening. So act normal. Talk about the good things. Give them a break. Even though you may want answers, they are living in it, and at times, distraction is much appreciated.

For spouses, partners, this is a team exercise. When the relationship started, I knew I wanted the best care for Brianna. In my mind, the geniuses of Brianna and her disease were her parents. They were the experts. Having them there helped. If Brianna was trying to remember something about her past, they were there. They knew everything from birth on.

Brianna and I had some very difficult situations. But they weren't Brianna's fault, nor mine. They were life struggles. My career.

CF issues. Just because our story seems like such an amazing fairy tale doesn't mean we didn't have struggles, conflict, or tough times. But getting through those challenges made us stronger. What's important is how you adjust, love, and lean on each other for support. Be honest, clear, and always working toward a better life. Be creative. It affects both of you, but they live with it. Most likely they feel the same way you do, but they are overwhelmed by it. Think of ways to help instead of pointing out ways they can do better. A few times, Brianna would start doing things because she wanted to do them and wouldn't allow me to do them, even though she knew I was doing them out of the kindness of my heart. Never hold grudges about anything, but always build a better team, constantly readdressing feelings, both positive and negative. Brianna and I never shied away from being vocal and making clear what things made us feel good. Everyone is fast to criticize but compliments go so much farther. If we missed something, those pillow talks usually allowed us a chance to address them.

Our entire journey, we both felt open to sharing our thoughts and feelings about her CF. She felt the same way I did, but that was our reality. We talked about it from the beginning. Some people have a difficult time talking about illness, but they figure out ways to be a part of helping their partner. Sometimes, the team behind the patient can be so uplifting and make the struggle so much easier. All of life is easier when you have a full group of people who love you and are rooting you on. Thank them.

Many times, I felt like getting mad at cystic fibrosis. I wished I could take it from Bri. But she looked at all experiences as a way to build character—and CF was just one of those relationships that kept her humble, powerful beyond measure, and really, it was a friendship she was always thankful for. At the celebration, Dr. Rosenfeld recalled a time when a medical student asked Bri if she wished she could not have had CF. Brianna thought for a while only to master her words, then said, "Honestly, no. Having CF is a part of what makes me who I am. It's taught me the power of the love of my family; it gives me a perspective about living each day to its fullest."

I remember Brittany, Brianna's best friend, once talking with Brianna about starting a video blog. Brittany lifted up Claire Wineland's video blogs. One of Claire's strongest messages was, "Stop pitying them and empower them." Britt showed me a video in which Claire said, "When you pity people who are sick, you take away their power." Embrace their independence; don't take it away. Encourage it.

Thankfully, Brianna started a few video blogs. She had never posted them, but they have been very therapeutic for me to watch. I continue to learn from her.

Another huge thing Brianna and I worked on a lot was communication. Every time I go to work, my dad constantly drills me with, "Think about what you say before you say it; think about what you do before you do it." That's something Brianna and I did too. Think about how you say things. Consider, "Brianna is dying of cystic fibrosis" versus "Brianna is living with cystic fibrosis." There's a big difference. Brianna was always positive, so she saw it as the latter.

Our knowledge is usually our worst enemy. We fear what we know. We are diagnosed with a terminal disease, and sometimes, this comes with a set or restrictions. We all have an hourglass; only some have a sense of how much sand is left, while others are completely oblivious. Why can't we live like kids? Lacking the knowledge to fear makes them fearless, determined; with no idea what monsters are lurking, they live without fear.

Brianna loved everyone and loved to give. So much so that she was continuously buying people gifts because she loved to see them smile. We even had a spot in the garage where she gathered gifts until she found the perfect opportunity to gift them. Anything from framed lyrics she handwrote to people's unique, favorite items. From small gifts to her amazing presence, she gave every single person she met a piece of her light, then walked even brighter than when she came in.

CF did not take Brianna; her devotion to God did. Indeed, Brianna was a special one. Through this amazing journey, she remained devoted to God. I have struggled with my faith. Being an engineer, and a scientific mind, I am conflicted; I have questions. But Brianna didn't judge me on that; she continued teaching by example. My mom's journey to heaven, and especially Brianna's, has definitely made me believe in the power of Christ; it has made it impossible to deny his existence. That a person of Brianna's beauty could have control of her life in such a struggle—there is no way to deny she was a product of God. I often play her copy of "God Must Have Spent a Little More Time on You" by Alabama. It was true. Brianna was definitely proof of God.

A year after Brianna passed, on July 11, 2018, our seventh wedding anniversary—yes another seven—I got a tattoo on the inside of my right forearm as a constant reminder of her presence. Brittany got a tattoo of Brianna's quote in Brianna's handwriting, which we had pulled from one of Brianna's journals, "Choose your attitude, create your life" on her arm, and she encouraged me to get my first tattoo and for it to be the same. I couldn't resist. To personalize it, in full blue and green, I added a peacock feather. It meant so much. Later, in December, I got a tattoo on my left arm representing my mother, with trees for the northwest, and a trail leading the way to mom's favorite poem "Footprints in the Sand." My two girls were now holding my hands through life. The tattoos are visible as a constant reminder that I am always walking with the two most inspirational people in my life. Brianna's tattoo is a constant reminder of her encouraging words and a great way to continue her legacy by sharing her amazing story—and my love for her. It also offers me her amazing support in the toughest times when I read it. And who would have guessed it would be on the eleventh anniversary of our first date that I got our tattoo.

However, I was shocked to find some people were conflicted about the tattoos. They meant a lot to me, but some people were uncomfortable with their emotions, or the topic of death, so they got weird about the tattoos or my explanation of them. They are on the inside of my forearms, easy for me to see, but also easy for others to see and question. Conflicted, anxious to build friendships, I have held my story back. It doesn't always feel right to share.

It's been a struggle. Death is something that people place in a negative space, an uncomfortable space, but for me, it was so beautiful, and actually brought comfort. Sharing it has been a struggle. We don't heal from a loved one's death; we just learn how to adapt, how to store the pain of their absence. It's like people want you to be sad, but not overbearing in sharing it. They want you to be happy, but not so happy that you act like nothing is wrong. You have to move on, but any sign of moving on makes it look like the loss is not a big deal. I was lost—confused. My feelings felt valid, but they weren't received as such. In these situations, heck, everyone's feelings are valid because it's a lot to deal with. We need to be constantly understanding of others for their actions because they hurt and are dealing with things the best way they know how. No matter how we cope, the person we lose is always a part of our past, a part of who we are, so we must accept that such a loss affects everyone differently. Personally, I felt out of place, emotionally disconnected from people. I was lost. I wanted to share Brianna's story—my story.

Stuck in a struggle to understand, trying to find my footing, trying to find myself, I finally found the answer. After two years, I woke up one day and my eyes were extremely milky and hurt. I was supposed to go to breakfast with a friend, and I forced myself through it. But it was a lot to overcome. Trying not to panic, I continued on. About midday, I tried to go work out. Working out was my new release and mental therapy.

As I was walking to the gym, I stopped to blow my nose. Instead of coming out of my nose, all the air escaped the left side of my lip. I had no control of the left side of my lip. Trying not to panic, I grabbed my phone and turned the camera on myself, using my high-tech mirror app. The left side of my face was completely paralyzed. My left eyebrow did not move; my left eye did not close; the left side of my mouth did not retain air.

I went to the worst possible place to investigate my symptoms—Dr. Google. Everything I read said stroke. I panicked. Thankfully, my doctor is a close friend, so I reached out, racing to his clinic.

Bell's palsy.

Bell's palsy is an inflamed nerve on the side of the face, usually caused by a virus. Later, I learned other parts of my body would have been affected if it were a stroke. Who would have known Bell's palsy was such a common uncommon thing? Luckily, things, for the most part, have returned to normal. But it was a huge wakeup call!

Right after Brianna passed, I talked with many people about how amazing her story was, and I knew it was just a matter of time before I had to share it with the world. But losing Brianna has been difficult. I've been struggling to find my footing, trying to live again.

That day when I realized half my face was paralyzed, it reminded me about how fragile life is. It reminded me that today is all I have. It reminded me of the true value of Brianna's legacy. It was as if Brianna were there in person, once again sharing her love, resetting, encouraging me, giving me a swift kick in the butt. I needed to start working on her story, to start sharing her legacy. To embrace it. To embrace my tattoos and their true meaning. To tell the real story. Even if people are uncomfortable. Life should be something we are supposed to celebrate. I needed to share the story to help others, instead of neglecting the power of Brianna's story.

Brianna never feared anything because she knew she lived every day to the fullest. No matter how difficult the road ahead was, even with a death sentence in the form of CF, she was going to cram her life with positivity. Hope. Love. Family. Empathy. Now. Because of this, even at 20 percent lung function, she lived all twenty-nine years she was given—sixteen more years than CF's original sentence of thirteen years of age. She was simply choosing to live. The entire time I was loving someone who was living. But while being aware of the reality that we are all dying, she focused on living, not allowing one minute to be overlooked because she craved a quality life. Like the song she had me play at the end of her celebration to get everyone up and dancing, happily we shout that we are alive; we feel alive; we are dancing on God's great dance floor.

We can keep Brianna's legacy alive, leading to a brighter tomorrow, no matter the struggle. As a true BriLiever, whenever you are in a situation, big or small, just ask yourself, "What would Brianna do on her great dance floor?"

Yes, this is our story, Brianna's story, but your story isn't any different! You can also choose to leave a legacy! To live is a choice. Life is full of choices for us to make. And we are completely in control of each and every choice, no matter the status of our journey. It's how we overcome our challenges and struggles in life, no matter the level of tragedy. Our past is forever unchangeable, but our future is always a choice away, while we never know if tomorrow will ever come. We are all humans; no one is perfect, but we are all perfectly imperfect. As Brianna said in her speech, "Life has a certain ending, but an uncertain timing." The distance between when we were born and our death will only be known on our headstone, but the dash between we have control over. We can control the story it tells, and the legacy it shares. As time runs out for all of us, and days go by, make sure you take your dash via her legacy, and like Brianna did,

Choose your attitude,
create your life!

always,
Brianna

RESOURCES

Bri and I always dreamed to be geniuses; however, we didn't like to make up things. So in our best interest, of making facts not fiction, we used the following resources to check in from time to time to make sure we were steering in the right direction.

- Colleen Hitchcock's poem "Ascension"

- CF Foundation: National and Seattle Chapters. CFF.org/Washington

- "Laying Siege to a Deadly Disease." *Time Magazine.* February 24, 1992, 139.8.

- Seattle Children's Hospital. SeattleChildrens.org

- *The Documentary.* Claire Wineland. YouTube.

- UW Pulmonary Clinic—Dr. Dandekar

- UW First Year Class—Dr. Rosenfeld

- UW Infectious Disease—Dr. Pottinger

- Washington State & National Future Farmers of America. WashingtonFFA.org

- Centers for Disease Control and Prevention. CDC.gov

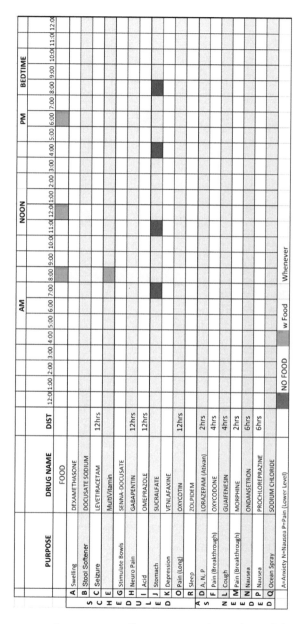

	PURPOSE	DRUG NAME	DIST	AM			NOON			PM		BEDTIME
		FOOD										
A	Swelling	DEXAMETHASONE										
B	Stool Softener	DOCUSATE SODIUM										
C	Seizure	LEVETIRACETAM	12hrs									
E		MultiVitamin										
G	Stimulate Bowls	SENNA-DOCUSATE										
H	Neuro Pain	GABAPENTIN	12hrs									
I	Acid	OMEPRAZOLE	12hrs									
J	Stomach	SUCRALFATE										
K	Depression	VENLAFAXINE										
O	Pain (Long)	OXYCOTIN	12hrs									
R	Sleep	ZOLPIDEM										
D	A, N, P	LORAZEPAM (Ativan)	2hrs									
F	Pain (Breakthrough)	OXYCODONE	4hrs									
L	Cough	GUAIFENESIN	4hrs									
M	Pain (Breakthrough)	MORPHINE	2hrs									
N	Nausea	ONDANSETRON	6hrs									
P	Nausea	PROCHLORPERAZINE	6hrs									
Q	Ocean Spray	SODIUM CHLORIDE										

A=Anxiety N=Nausea P=Pain (Lower Level)

NO FOOD | w Food | Whenever

For your convenience, a complimentary excel template of this Medical Schedule Sheet is available at **ChooseYourAttitude.org/Resources**

247

LEARN MORE ABOUT
BRIANNA

This book is full of BriMazing info. In addition to the photo inserts in this book, visit **ChooseYourAttitude.org/BriMazing** where you can find videos of her BriMazing speeches, as well as many items, including:

- 2007 Washington State FFA Retiring Address – Days Go By

- 2017 Senate Speech

- 2011 UW Q/A

- Her *Time Magazine* cover

- End of Life Celebration Video

- Articles/Newspaper Clippings

- Picture Archive

Along with these videos and transcripts, many other resources can be found at **ChooseYourAttitude.org**.

WHAT'S YOUR
BRIMAZING
EXPERIENCE?

Have you been affected directly by
Brianna's amazingness?
Well, share it with the world!

We want to hear it! Or just come see what
others have to share!

Log onto
ChooseYourAttitude.org/BriMazing
and click
Share Your BriMazing!

CHOOSE YOUR
ATTITUDE

Besides Brianna's amazing legacy, at Choose Your Attitude, we have come together, led by Nicholas and Brianna's Best Friend, Brittany, with a team of others high off of BriMazing, to help others live amazing lives like Brianna did. Through Choose Your Attitude, we focus on three things: Past, Present, Future.

- **PAST:** Helping people who have lost loved ones, in dealing with and overcoming the grief, pain, and tragedy of that loss.

- **PRESENT:** Helping inspire people through ailment, disease, challenge (sexual abuse, criminal behavior, eating disorders, drug or alcohol addiction, sexual identity conflict, etc.), or making the journey of life much more life-fulfilling, whether it be the person directly going through it, and/or the friends, family, or anyone around you.

- **FUTURE:** Maybe you haven't dealt with death, an ailment, a struggle, or tragedy directly, but you are looking to be inspired, and want tools to overcome potential challenges and live a life of legacy like Brianna.

By taking all three of these into consideration, we hope to share Brianna's journey, create products and workshops to help people through life, and help everyone take what life has given them, no matter what life has led them through, and transform it into something beautiful and life fulfilling. Embrace your past as it makes for a brighter future. Everyone deserves to be loved, and everyone has a choice to live while we all are dying. So we all practice Brianna's advice: "Choose your attitude, create your life!"

Podcasts, Shop, Resources, Much More!

Check Us Out!

 Follow Us

#ChooseAttitudeCreateLife

CHOOSEYOURATTITUDE.ORG

SHOP
CHOOSE YOUR ATTITUDE

Come visit us at SHOP Choose Your Attitude where we have:
Resources to help inspire,
Tools to apply yourself and engage,
and Apparel to scream to the world!

<u>Apparel Shop</u>
T-Shirts, Hoodies, Jackets, Hats

<u>Books & More</u>
Loving Someone Who Is Dying
Quotes On A Fridge
Journals, Stickers, Bookmarks, Cards, Water Bottles

We are always creating!
So check back in for new additions!
If you have an idea, share it with us!
We would love to help make it a reality!

ChooseYourAttitude.org/Shop

QUOTES ON A FRIDGE

Authors: Brianna Oas Strand & Nicholas Strand
Illustrator: Pat Bradley

The *Quotes on a Fridge* book shares the journey of Brianna and her obsession with quotes. Brianna's life was challenging, but one of her many ways to help her rise up every morning, no matter her struggle, was placing quotes all over, constantly inviting you to be inspired and often laugh. *Quotes on a Fridge* brings you through this journey, shares a number of her many favorite quotes, and helps lead you to follow her and inspire yourself in the comfort of your own home and the world around you. Life is difficult, but Brianna shares with you how making a little step can help you make a large impact.

And this is just the beginning of a series!

So order now, and watch for more coming soon!

SHOP NOW

ChooseYourAttitude.org/QuotesOnAFridge

ABOUT THE AUTHOR

NICHOLAS STRAND is an author, professional keynote speaker, life coach, and entrepreneur, who is passionate about living. Driven, motivated, and inspired, Nick uses his love and passion for his late wife Brianna to continue her legacy, to help others deal with death and cope with illnesses, overcome tragedy, to spread cystic fibrosis and infectious disease antibiotic-resistance awareness, and to live life to the fullest, working toward Brianna's dream of making CF stand for Cure Found.

Nick married the love of his life, and walked with her on her amazing journey of battling cystic fibrosis and mycobacterium abscessus until she went to heaven. With a soul so strong and bright, yet a body that could not keep up, Brianna left an amazing legacy, which Nick uses to continue her drive to help others. From speaking to people about death and how to love someone who is dying to encouraging people to live life to the fullest, Nick is driven to make Brianna proud! Since creating the organization Choose Your Attitude, he has been constantly busy. Now that *Loving Someone Who Is Dying* is completed, he has a number of other projects planned, including a second book. In addition, by continually speaking on the topic of Choose Your Attitude, Nick hopes to continue sharing his wife's amazing legacy and creating meaning for others to overcome their own many levels of tragedy.

Nick started his entrepreneurial career in the audio-visual industry where he is a video engineer, LED technician, and video system designer by day in the music concert touring industry. He has worked on video displays for performers like Kelly Clarkson, Maroon 5, Kanye West, Stevie Wonder, Rush, the Dave Matthews Band, Sting, and Tom Petty—just to name a few.

Combining it all together, taking every day as it comes, Nick is constantly reminded of his wife's amazing words:

Choose your attitude,
create your life!

always,
Brianna

BOOK NICK TO SPEAK AT YOUR NEXT EVENT

By embracing Brianna's legacy, Nick Strand has found a new journey in life: helping to inspire others through living a full life! From his many years of living his dream career on the road by touring as a video engineer to learning to love someone who is dying and dealing with grief post-losing someone, Nick has pulled himself out of darkness by sharing his story, his love for Brianna, and his success in living his dream career. Today, he gains fuel and inspiration of his own by helping everyone else live such a full and prosperous life through the new organization Choose Your Attitude and speaking behind Choose Your Attitude, Create Your Life! From speaking engagements and workshops to continually adding to the resources available to help everyone through life's journey, Nick is constantly looking for ways to help others deal with struggles we have no control over and make the best of them. You, too, can Choose Your Attitude, Create Your Life! And Nick can help you get there!

Nick is available to speak and assist in the following ways:

- Life Coaching
- Book Marketing/Publishing Coach
- Public Speaking: Choose Your Attitude, Create Your Life

Book Nick today! Lead your team to a brighter future!

Speaking@ChooseYourAttitude.org
NicholasStrand.com
ChooseYourAttitude.org/Speaking

ON A WHIM, BRIANNA CONVINCED HER DAD TO TAKE PICTURES WITH HER HORSE IN HER WEDDING DRESS. SHE HAD A 101° TEMPERATURE AND HAD HER 24 HOUR IV REMOVED FOR THE DURATION OF THE SHOOT. LATER, THE PICTURE BECAME THE ICONIC COVER PHOTO.

NICHOLAS STRAND

Brianna Oas Strand

Choose your attitude, create your life!

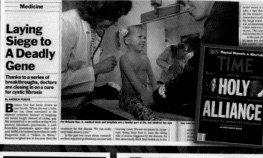

Medicine

Laying Siege to A Deadly Gene

Thanks to a series of breakthroughs, doctors are closing in on a cure for cystic fibrosis

By ANDREW PURVIS

Sparks Fly

Nick & Brianna post convention

Brianna RA stage

07' WA State Officer Team

Washington FFA

LOVE IS IN THE AIR

CF Gala 07'

Nick & Bri with Justin & Erica

Always being silly

family

Nephew Jack & Bri

Rylee & Bri

Texas trip to WA with Justin

Mom's last photoshoot, a week before she passed

Nick & Brianna
Dating & Engagement

Our first photoshoot 2008

Go Hawks!

Out with friends

Vegas trip

Just Married

Honeymoon
IN JAMAICA ♥

Dolce

Bentley

Celery

Souie

Frisbee & Apple

Dolce

BRI'S SCHOOLING & VETERINARY WORK

Practice Manager

Dr. Maci & Brianna

Dr. Jasmine & Bri

Nick welcomed Brianna
from her last class of college
with gifts and WSU fight song

NICK'S WORK

CYSTIC FIBROSIS

To a kid, Cystic Fibrosis sounds like . . .

65 Roses

Big Bro Justin taking care of Brianna

Nebulizer

Hospital visit with Larry the I.V. Machine

Constant affection for food!

Brianna

Public Speaking

Honor Society 2016
STRANDER PHOTOGRAPHY SmugMug.com

D.C. Senate 2017

Head of the Table

Capitol Building Tour

WASHINGTON, D.C. TRIP

Nick, Brianna, Justin and Val

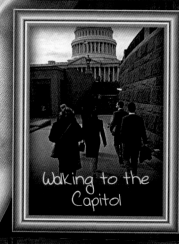
Walking to the Capitol

Bri at the Smithsonian

The struggle behind the smile.

FRAGILE MOMENTS

BRIANNA'S LAST DAYS

Bri with her best friends

May 6, 2017 - Day before

Making a dash from the hospital

Sun shining on Bri watching her neice Rylee

Kristen getting Bri ready to go home

Saying goodbye

Last visit with Dolce at the farm